Other Books by Wayne Karlin:

Novels:

Crossover
Lost Armies
The Extras
Us

Anthologies:

THE OTHER SIDE OF HEAVEN: Postwar Fiction by Vietnamese and American Writers (co-edited with Le Minh Khue and Truong Vu)

FREE FIRE ZONE: Short Stories by Vietnam Veterans (co-edited with Basil T. Paquet and Larry Rottman)

RUMORS AND STONES

A JOURNEY

by
Wayne Karlin

CURBSTONE PRESS

Printed in the U.S. on acid-free paper by BookCrafters
Cover design: Stone Graphics
Special thanks to Jane Blanshard for help in preparing this book.

Curbstone Press is a 501(c)(3) nonprofit publishing house whose programs are supported in part by private donations and by grants from: ADCO Foundation, Witter Bynner Foundation for Poetry, Connecticut Commission on the Arts, Connecticut Arts Endowment Fund, The Ford Foundation, The Greater Hartford Arts Council, Junior League of Hartford, Lawson Valentine Foundation, LEF Foundation, Lila Wallace-Reader's Digest Literary Publishers Marketing Development Program administered by CLMP, The Andrew W. Mellon Foundation, National Endowment for the Arts, Puffin Foundation, and United Way-Windham Region.

Library of Congress Cataloging-in-Publication Data

    Karlin, Wayne.
      Rumors and stones : a journey / by Wayne Karlin. — 1st ed.
        p. cm.
      ISBN 1-880684-42-X
      1. Karlin, Wayne—Journeys—Poland—Kolno (Lomza)
      2. Jews—Poland—Kolno (Lomza)—Biography.
      3. Holocaust, Jewish (1939-1945)—Poland—Kolno
      (Lomza). 4. Kolno (Lomza, Poland)—History. I. Title.
    DS135.P62K6643   1996
    940.53'18—dc20   96-22226

published by
CURBSTONE PRESS   321 Jackson St.   Willimantic, CT 06226
    e-mail: curbston@connix.com
    WWW: www.connix.com/~curbston/

With special thanks
to the Maryland State Arts Council
and the National Endowment for the Arts,
without whose support this book would not have been
completed, to Ohnmar, as always, and to Michael Glaser
for his compassionate insights and suggestions

ACKNOWLEDGMENTS

Several sections of this book, in different form, have appeared in *Free Fire Zone, Glimmer Train, Passager, Swords into Ploughshares, Vietnam Forum* and *The Vietnam War in American Stories, Songs and Poems.* The author would also like to thank the following people and credit the following publications: Lucille Clifton, George Evans, Larry Heinemann, and Bruce Weigl for excerpts from their work; *The Kolno Memorial Book,* published by the Yad Vashem Holocaust Memorial, Jerusalem, Israel; *The Orbis Guide Book,* published by the Polish Tourist Agency; *The Survivor* and *Writing into the World,* by Terrence Des Pres; *Class Struggle in the Pale,* by Ezra Mendelsohn. Epigraphs from *The Drowned and the Saved* by Primo Levi reprinted with the permission of Simon & Schuster; copyright 1968 by Guillio Einaudi editores s.p.s., Torino; translation copyright 1988 by Simon & Schuster, Inc.; epigraphs from *Four Hours in My Lai* by Michael Bilton and Kevin Sim used by permission of Viking Penguin, a division of Penguin Books USA Inc.

For Adam
and
For those who couldn't fly

CONTENTS

ones like us

enter a blurry world
fetish tight around our
smallest finger, mezuzah
gripped in our good child hand.
we feel for our luck
but everywhere is menace menace
until we settle ourselves
against the bark of trees, against
the hide of fierce protection
and there, in the shadow,
words call us. words call us
and we go.

Lucille Clifton

RUMORS AND STONES

PROLOGUE

THE JOURNEY

JULY, 1993

In the summer of 1993 I began a self-imposed journey
into the blurred space between memory, story and
reality when I rented a car from Warsaw Avis and drove
to the village in Poland in which my mother had lived
before emigrating to the United States. It was a trip I
had mixed feelings about making. I felt a sense of
obligation and curiosity—my mother had died two
years before and had talked often about Kolno, though
she never wanted to go back to it and didn't know what
had happened to the town or her remaining relatives
after she'd left. Since her death, I'd found out that in July
of 1941 all the Jews of Kolno, two thousand men,
women and children, had been lined up at the edge of
trenches and machine gunned to death by the
Germans—an image that became linked in my mind

with My Lai. The murders had occurred with the often enthusiastic help of many of the local Poles. These people or their descendants now lived in the village, and I didn't know if I wanted to be among them.

There were other reasons for my ambivalence. My father had died when I was five and so had always been a story, a mythical archetype in my life, and my mother was already in danger of becoming another one: her stories had entered a realm that I feared to erode with reality. On the other hand, it was just that imaginative tension that I wanted to explore. My mother had been a slight woman who lived fiercely and regarded the world with bitter wariness and knowledge: she had a survivor's understanding that to save one's life one needed to reinvent it.

The Vietnamese, I'd come to learn, had a custom of sometimes hiding their true names behind nicknames in order to misdirect malevolent spirits, a *k'ain ahora*— a way of putting off the evil eye. My mother lived in similar shells of identity: her given, Hebrew name Rachel, Ruhu, kerneled into Rhoda, her jet-black hair camouflaged to platinum blond. She'd come to America when she was fourteen, but the year of her arrival and her age at the time both changed fluidly as she got older—the former advanced while the latter retreated. After her death I found papers in her safe deposit box— her citizenship papers and a letter from the New York Public School system that stated she'd completed eighth grade. The papers not only added ten years to the age she'd claimed, but also placed her actual day of birth in a completely different month than the one we'd been celebrating all my life. There was no reason for the latter deception I could think of except as a refugee's tic, an automatic and compulsive need to create a fictional identity.

I wondered what other elements in the stories she'd told me had been changed and distorted, though I was not particularly shocked or disillusioned by her action—I was, after all, a writer of fictions, by definition someone who lied in order to tickle out some sort of truth. But I had been in the Vietnam war and had written books and stories about its aftermath, and I was sometimes troubled by my efficacy and motivation in bending that situation and its real deaths to the shapings and twists of fiction.

Perhaps some of the motivations behind my mother's flawed rememberings—conscious or not— were obvious and commonplace. She wanted to be younger, richer; she wanted to be a dispossessed princess; she wanted me and others to sense an echo of doomed and tragic glamour under the tediousness of her life She wanted, mainly, to change the past so that she could be forgiven and could forgive herself for the present: that is, she wanted what everybody wanted. Her parents had been rich, she told me: her mother never lifted a finger, even sent all her children to a Polish wet nurse. The family was so poor, she told me, they had to beg potatoes from the peasants and nearly starved one winter. Her father, she told me, was a man who, while not a religious fanatic, was so learned in the Talmud that rich men and rabbis would come to him for advice. Her father was a kind of doctor, she said. Her father was a smuggler, she said—the village of Kolno was near the German border and her father and brothers would sometimes smuggle horses across, sometimes linen and fine cloth.

How could Kolno be near the German border? My own birth certificate listed my mother's birthplace as Russia, which meant the village had to be located in the Pale, that area of eastern Poland that had been under Russian sovereignty until the 1930s, and in which the Jews, who made up the majority of the population, were segregated by law and self-segregated by custom, language and desire. No, it was near Germany, she insisted. She had a number of photographs from Europe: I would stare at them hungrily when I was a child, bits of physical evidence, as real as stones. One was of her father, stern, bearded, narrow-faced—dressed in black silk. One was of an arched window against a black background, a sign with Hebrew letters centered in one pane. A third was of my mother, her mother and her younger brother grouped around her father's grave in the Kolno cemetery. It was a picture taken, she told me, just before they left for America. At the base of the gravestone, a number of smaller stones had been placed to provide solid evidence of their visit, as is the Jewish custom.

RUMORS

In the game called Rumors, a sentence is created and whispered into the ear of the first child sitting in a row. He whispers what he heard into the ear of the next child, and the next, until, finally, the last child repeats the sentence out loud. It is always changed. The hard facts of it have passed from mouth to ear to mouth, been filtered through different perceptions and experiences and imaginations, and in this passage it has become rimed with all the truths it has seeped through, so that when the last child tells the story, it has become more than itself. It has become the story of everyone through whom it has passed.

This is the way it was with my mother's stories: they grew from the real world while at the same time they were like dreams or rumors, their codes locked in her own references and memories, more riddles than guides. I never knew what to trust. I live now in a part of Maryland where solid proofs of the past are everywhere: Indian arrowheads, settlers' middens, the bones of Confederate soldiers and Piscataway Indians and English tobacco planters suddenly poking through the exposed roots and red mud of the steep riverbank as if time were turning over in its sleep to show its other side. But my mother got on a ship and, after its departure, her world burned. A few photographs are the only physical evidence it ever existed.

The photograph is like a picture of a memory: it has a crack running through it, and its images have faded to a dark sepia. It is pasted on an oblong piece of crumbling cardboard. On the other side of the cardboard is a page cut from a Polish newspaper, two columns of words bisected raggedly by a tear whose edges have been taped together. The words make the cracked, hardened paper into an undeciphered Rosetta stone. In the photograph, my grandmother, my mother and my mother's youngest brother are standing around my grandfather's grave in Poland. The gravestone is inscribed with Hebrew words, two columns of them, like the columns of the newspaper on the other side. Like the words on the other side, these also tease rather than illuminate; they form a puzzle in which my grandfather is locked. The mended tear in the paper locks the other figures in the photo into the same puzzle. Dressed in black, bent over or standing straight, they are as mysterious as letters in an alien alphabet.

My mother, a slight girl of twelve or thirteen, has a black hood half-hiding her thin face. She stands behind the gravestone. She looks so pale that she seems to be growing from it. During the last year of he life, she dreamt that stone, felt its coldness growing inside herself. She did not accept the steadily increasing failures of her body with grace or with peace, but rather fought them with an astonished bitterness, as if she were the only person to whom this had ever happened. She fought with a growing abrasiveness directed at her second husband and sometimes at me, a sharp-edge of criticism and complaint that let us know she was still there. And she fought with her stories.

Her mother bore thirteen children, though many of them died at birth. Once, fearing that my grandmother's sanity would tip, the midwife took the dead child away, heated a stone, wrapped it in swaddling and brought it to her. My grandmother pressed its warmth to her breast until it turned cold and then knowing it was a stone, perhaps feeling its weight on her like the weight of the stillborn come outside her body, she still pressed it to her, as if she wanted to suckle it to life. In the photograph, her face as sharply cut as a cardboard silhouette, her head also hooded in black, she is kneeling by the side of the diminutive grassy mound of the grave. An air of impatience has been caught in the slightly strained awkwardness of her position, or perhaps in a slight upturn of her mouth; it is as if she had become as skeptical about death as she were about birth.

Her husband, my grandfather, smuggled cloth and other goods from Germany to Poland in order to support his family. Sometimes he had his daughters wrap the material around their bodies; once over the border they would open their dresses and pull out, as if with midwives' hands, shapeless masses of gleaming linen, yards of silk that shivered like new skin. Yet in spite of the smuggling, my grandfather was a man learned in the Talmud and was also, my mother believed, a kind of doctor; that is, he did something, she told me, with people's eyes. People who wanted to go to America would come to him and he'd check their eyes with a candle and sign a paper. What did the paper signify? What exactly did he do? I wanted to know, but my mother wasn't sure. She only knew that people would come to the house and he would seat them in the parlor and draw the heavy, velvet curtain. The room would be dark as night. He would light the candle and hold it up to their faces, the way a flame is put next to an egg to see the life curled inside, as if he could see the soul itself.

My mother's younger brother, who in the photo stands to the right of the grave wearing a student's cap, a high-collared tunic, and leggings, became a movie projectionist in America. The RKO theatre on Main Street in White Plains where he worked was not some cramped multiplex box. Its high walls were painted a rich, Victorian drawing room red, their angles and seams crusted with gilt curlicues and ornate scroll work. Massive box balconies that no one ever sat in hung on each side of the screen, and a thirty to forty row deep balcony sloped down from the rear wall. The screen itself was a great expanse of waiting blankness, stained by suggestive shapes as if by the residue of visions and memories. My uncle would take me with him to the very top of the theatre, to the sanctum of the projection booth—a dark, cool chamber that you entered with the sense of coming into a mind. In that pragmatic room of black metal beams and gray concrete floor hidden in the forehead of the red and gold temple, I would watch him work the heavy mechanism: the clicking, clanking, whirring contraption of cylinders and reels and celluloid that created dreams and stories. I would stand in the flickering darkness and watch through the slit-like window as he cast his light onto the blank eye of the screen, just as my grandfather would shine his light into the eyes of those who would go to America. Together we would watch how the light revealed the visions behind that white eye.

The year before we moved from Manhattan to White Plains, television came onto our block like a very subtle secret agent, offering no hint of the revolution it had come to effect. Small, unobtrusive screens appeared in two or three apartments in our building on 96th Street near Amsterdam Avenue, the way relatives from Europe would appear in my father's apartment on Henry Street when he was a boy. He would wake up, and they would be there, their forms and arguments and joys suddenly and seamlessly attached to the forms and arguments and joys of his family, as if they wanted to pretend they had always been there. My father would watch their eyes open on their first day in America and wonder what they saw—just as I sat in our neighbor's living room and watched someone turn a knob, a blink like an eye opening and did not have to wonder, for I saw the images etched onto that eye: shadowy gray shapes, ghosts of other lives and worlds—that eye looking inwards at its own dreams.

When I came back from our neighbor's apartment, laughing and excited, bursting to tell my mother what I had witnessed, she looked at me, her face wary with a knowledge that carved the joy out of the morning, a certainty that this event was simply another trap the world was laying for her. Over that year, I had watched her face take on lines of bitterness as if it were being poured into the mold of her own mother's face in the photograph she kept on the dresser bureau: herself as a girl standing with my grandmother and uncle around my grandfather's grave in Poland, a place and people about whom she would try to tell me stories, stories I did not want to hear, especially just then. That day, when I saw that she was going to respond to my discovery with a story, I turned and ran away, fleeing whatever knowledge about the world those faces in the photograph held, holding tightly inside me instead that small, bright, boxed image I had brought upstairs, even as I would try to hold onto a good dream in the hard light of day.

I ran. Outside, my father was skipping rope on the sidewalk in front of the building, his face hard and concentrated, the rope whizzing viciously, whipping the concrete with sharp pings, the empty, pinned-up left leg of his trousers bobbing up and down, so I could sense an invisible leg extending muscularly from it, a ghost of a foot just missing the whirling rope. My father saw me and smiled reassuringly, but he did not stop jumping. Even with one leg, he still skipped rope with a beautiful precision. In his late teens and early twenties he had been a light heavyweight, one of that generation of tough, quick Eastside Jews who had dominated boxing for a time. But he had given up fighting, except for coaching Golden Gloves, when he married my mother, and I have no memory of him boxing or of very much else about him. The only picture I carry in my mind is of my father skipping rope on one leg in front of our building that day, his face grim and concentrated and tight with pain, as if he were getting himself ready for an opponent who would give him the fight of his life.

The Haskell apartment where I saw my first television set was in the basement of our building on 96th Street. As my father grew more ill, my mother left me for longer and longer periods of time in that dark, pleasantly filthy series of rooms where Timmy and Kevin Haskell and I sat and watched Froggy plunk his magic twanger and Ramar the Jungle Boy. The Haskells were the only Christian family in the building. Mrs. Haskell was from Wisconsin, a pale and plump Nordic blonde deserted by her husband, a plumbing fixtures salesman. Her flaxen hair was out of place in that building of dark heads; her two boys were wild as Cossacks, good at fixing our bikes and building roller-skate-crate cars, good at stealing free rides on the back of buses. The smells of Haskell food and the sounds of Haskell laughter were strange to the rest of the families in the building. The other mothers whispered disgustedly about how Mrs. Haskell let her boys keep a pet white rat. Yet an empathy existed between my mother and Mrs. Haskell, as if they were both knit by some hard-binding knowledge of the world and its tricks, and my mother left me with her for hours and days as she went to the doctor and to the hospital. I played with the rat, or with Kevin and Timmy. But mostly, I sat in front of the television, so that what I see now, I see as if on that small screen, its picture blurred by the comfortable fur of dust that lay over everything in the Haskell's apartment.

I see my mother entering the doctor's office, her eyes so intense that his eyes flee their question, seek refuge in the intricacies of the dismantled television set on a table against one wall of the room, its parts laid out like the parts of a patient he couldn't figure out how to put back together. The doctor sits behind a large white desk, its surface bare except for a heavy black telephone. His office is floored with a white carpet so thick that my mother's movement across the floor is silent; her weight leaves impressions that stay for a second, then disappear as the fiber springs up, and she imagines suddenly all the patients and patients' relatives who have passed and left no trace on this carpet. The doctor looks back to my mother, his face furious. He is a thin, severe man with a pencil-line mustache. He was, by all accounts, phenomenally incompetent. In the beginning he misdiagnosed the tumor on my father's leg as a boil. When it metastasized, he amputated the leg, though by then it was too late. Even so, my parents kept coming to him. He was an American doctor; reputable, severe; they did not think to question his authority.

Have a seat, please.

My mother stands.

The doctor shrugs.

Your husband's new biopsy is back. He looks at her accusingly. I warned you not to hope for too much, that we may have waited too long to amputate.

My mother stares at the dismantled set. Yes, you were sure to warn me not to hope. The bitterness on her face twists her mouth into a small, triumphant smile; she is a prophet of doom who has been proven correct.

The telephone rings. The doctor looks at it with relief. Excuse me, he says, and picks it up. No, you're not, not at all, he says. I've been trying to get you all day. What? No, your man ran all the tests and said there was nothing more he could do. Then he just left, just like that. Listen, there's pieces everywhere, tubes and wires, a real mess.

He looks at my mother, as if inviting her to share his indignant disbelief. She is staring at him as if in fact she is doing just that. Her eyes are fixed on the telephone. Her hand reaches across the desk and snatches it from the doctor's hand. Holding it as if it were an ax, she draws it back and slashes at his face. A black crescent appears on his forehead over his welling eyes, and his head snaps back. A voice is yelling from the phone, although the doctor says nothing: it is as if his internal terror, once removed, is screaming from the telephone.

She smashes at the face of the man who has stolen pieces of her husband from her until he has disappeared from her life. My grandmother's face, in the photograph on the bureau back in our apartment, is as angry and bitter as my mother's face. She had buried six of her children in that same Polish soil into which she had just put her husband. He died of a stroke; before dying he had lost the use of his right arm. Bedridden for months, he was a terrible burden on a family trying to survive; if not for his illness, his wife and children would have left for America. On the day he died, he called my mother to his room and by sheer force of will drew his arm out of its death, as if out of a sleeve. He used it to point at the moon hanging outside the window. Now when she needs it, my mother feels the strength of that arm flow into her hand, the strength of her father to point the way to America, and the bitter strength of her mother's anger is burning in her arm and hand. The doctor crosses his hands in front of his face, and the telephone hits the back of his hands, a tiny, panicked voice screeching from it. She pounds at the doctor's face under his hands just as years later she will pound at the cold, empty face of her own death, drawing her strength from the stories that sat in her, as they sit in me, like anger.

RUMORS: DOV'S TOES

When my grandmother Sarah Gittel was halfway across the Atlantic on her way to America, she removed her Orthodox wig and threw it in the ocean. Then she shook her head rapidly, as if waking the crown of real hair she'd allowed to grow secretly under the wig. The hairs on the wig wriggled like the tentacles of a sea creature as it floated on the surface, until it soaked in the weight of the water and sank. She watched the disappearing black dot of the hairpiece with a smile that shocked her children as much as the action they'd just witnessed. It was a stranger's smile. It threw into doubt the whole country of memory.

Sarah Gittel wanted to leave some things behind, yet carry others. She carried a photograph of her husband's grave. In a linen handkerchief she kept tied around her neck as if it were an amulet, she carried two toes that belonged to her son Dov. He had left the family to join his older brothers Herman and Max and his older sisters Faigl and Bella, already in America, but every few months one of his comrades—he had been in a subversive organization—would deliver the money he sent from New York to their house in Kolno, the village where the family lived.

In spite of this evidence, Sarah Gittel worried about how her son, a cripple, was getting by in America. The year before, Dov had received word from a comrade who'd infiltrated the Ohkrana, the secret police, that he was to be drafted into the Russian army, a traditional way of getting rid of troublemakers.

On a cold winter morning a few days later, he bared his left foot and placed it on top of a stump behind the house. He looked up at the iron gray sky. Then he looked down at the gnarled stump sticking out from the smooth expanse of snow like something mutilated. Leaning against it was an ax. Dov broke the ax from the frozen grip of the ice, swung it over his head in a hissing arc, and brought it crashing down on the ice in the small trough next to the stump. It took two more blows to break a hole through the thick skin of ice. As soon as he saw the black water welling through, he gripped the ax up high on its handle with his right hand, touched the cold sharp blade to the area he wanted to hit, brought the ax up and then swung it down swiftly onto the stems of his two smallest toes. In the instant of the arc he saw himself frozen like a picture: a lean, intense man swinging an ax, his breath steaming in the air. The instant shattered like a shard of ice. He heard the solid chunk of the ax biting into the wood, felt it vibrate in his palms. He saw bright red blood gouting out onto white snow. The pain seared up his veins and lumped into throbbing, red-hot iron behind his eyes. Lifting his leg with both hands under the knee, he plunged his foot into the hole in the ice, which was already shrinking, then withdrew it. A blister of freezing blood formed around it. He sat on the stump and wrapped the foot in linen, then picked up the two pellets of his toes from the crusted snow. He wrapped them in some fine German linen he and his father had smuggled over the border the week before, and, using the ax for a crutch, limped back to the house.

Months afterwards, after he'd become involved in more radical politics and learned he was to be arrested anyway, he left the village. As he walked away, his mother came running down the road after him, holding the linen packet, screaming after him to take his toes, to take her, that he would need them both in America.

FIGHTS

I knew this about my father: when he was a young man
he was a professional boxer, a light-heavyweight. As a
child growing up in a neighborhood where the ability to
fight was important, I'd proudly shown the publicity
photos my mother had kept to the other kids, hoping
for some secondhand glory. In those pictures my father
was bare-chested, compact and strong, muscular arms
folded in easy menace, hands encased in boxing gloves,
his face leonine under tight golden curls, its
handsomeness redeemed by a broken nose. When he
was still a boxer, eighteen or nineteen or twenty years
old, he'd been married to an older woman, a rich but
barren middle-aged woman who had developed a
passion for him when she'd seen him fight. She'd
married him, took him out of the ring and the Henry
Street slum where he lived and put him into the
millinery business. The marriage, apparently, was
strained and strange and childless, and when my
mother, young and black-haired, with a thin, intense
beauty, came to work for him, something clicked
between them. She had a fire in her, her brothers would

say, with distressed awe. They'd brought her over to America like a memory of their European youth preserved in a photograph and then were disturbed when she looked around and took the country at its word. They wanted her to work for them as soon as she was old enough, but she got her own apartment, a railroad flat she shared with a girlfriend, and found her own work in the city, designing hats in the millinery trade, shaping cloth as once her smuggler father had shaped cloth to her body to bring it across borders. Already scandalized, the family ostracized her when she started seeing my father, a married man, an ex-boxer. My father's wife, however, didn't ignore her; she would appear whenever my mother went out with my father, burst into restaurants and Seventh Avenue showrooms, screaming curses and imprecations. Finally, since no rabbi would grant him a divorce so he could marry my mother, the two of them went to Mexico and did both.

They were people who crossed borders and rewrote themselves, as if after that first ocean crossing a fluidity had entered into their lives and any shape was possible and permitted. In Europe my mother was Rachel or Ruhu, and my paternal family name was Karlinsky. My father would have been a Talmudic scholar there—his grandfather was a famous rabbi—and a bride would have been found to match his brilliant lineage. In America, he changed his name and was chosen as if he were a virgin bride by a woman tapped into the power of the place; in America he became a boxer, as if the bobbing motion of prayer had been transmuted here.

Some of his friends, my mother said, were gangsters; they would visit him in his office. But my mother also told me that he was a trusting and generous man, and she always said this with a bitterness that made me believe it was true.

That's the end of the story, my mother said, we lived happily ever after until we didn't. What more do you want? What can I tell you? What other questions do you have?

She had left Kolno when she was twelve or thirteen or fourteen; as far as she knew we had no relatives left in the town during the Holocaust, a fact which was a bitter disappointment to me when I was a child (and which turned out to be wrong). The Holocaust obsessed me. I read everything about it I could get my hands on. I'm not entirely sure why the obsession came about, but I can guess at some of the reasons. My father's death when I was five had left us poor, though it was the kind of poor you didn't know you were until someone told you later. My mother, with her eighth-grade education and accented English, could only find work as a low-paid saleswoman in a White Plains dress store that sold very expensive dresses to very rich women. The development where we lived, Bryant Gardens (we had a small but comfortable one-bedroom apartment—I got the bedroom, my mother the couch), was analogous to her position: a working-class crescent of run-down two-story brick apartment buildings built behind the neighborhoods of single family homes and tree-shaded lawns like a reserve for those who served and dressed and maintained the dream. Only a few other Jewish families lived there. With my mother at the store, I was on my own all day after school, free as such kids are to invent my life, as many lives as I could: a solitary and strange reader drawn to the streets where I had the chance to act out some of the more weirdly appealing plot lines of the science-fiction and historical adventures and histories of the war I read. My friends for the most part were kids like me—their fathers gone to death, divorce or alcohol; a tribe whose territory was the alleys and basements, the abandoned garages where we snuck our first smokes and kissed our first girls, the parking lots and patch of woods behind the apartment buildings where we fought or played at war.

My war, though, wasn't always the same as theirs. I was the only Jew in the group and had my own slot: the other kids gleefully shooting their hands out in Nazi salutes, talking with mock-German accents, playing get-the-Jew games. *Riding through the Reich/in a black Mercedes Benz/Shooting all the Jews/Saving all my friends,* they'd sing with zest; was it the last or the next to the last line they were applying to me? I was troubled by the assumption I heard under their teasing that Jews were physical cowards, or at least somewhat nerdy—an important assumption when you lived in a place where acceptance often depended on how willing and able you were to use violence. It would seem strange to be bothered—my dad had been a boxer, my mother told me often, showing me his pictures in the ring—but I also knew that he hadn't been in a war, and the only other military service I'd heard about in my family involved one of her brothers, Herman, who, she thought, may have been with the Red Cavalry (a fact, a connection, that came back to me later, after Vietnam, when I discovered the stories of Isaac Babel, that Jew who had ridden like terror into Polish Jewish villages with Cossack horsemen in the name of a New World Order), and three older cousins—one had been a field surgeon in Belgium during the Second World War, the other a supply sergeant (these were both her brother David's sons), and the third had been wounded in the Battle of the Bulge. It may seem even stranger now that a child would be so concerned or obsessed with the most elemental definition of courage that participation in military service involved, and indeed at school I noticed that kids from the more cushioned neighborhoods, the kids I never saw later in Vietnam, seemed divorced from this concern. But in Bryant Gardens, war was the reference and basis for our play and our mythology, and World War II, finished ten years by my tenth birthday, was the backdrop of our childhood. It seeped into our language and consciousness from relatives who had been in it, from all the war movies of the fifties: Audie Murphy and Van Hefflin and John Wayne and Vic Morrow and his squad on the smaller screen of the television; its violence— legitimized, adult, well-equipped—fascinated us. Unfortunately, the images from it that seemed to apply to me, were images of helpless victimization, lines of people marching unresisting to gas chambers and ovens. There was much to read about the Holocaust then: *The Diary of Anne Frank* and John Hersey's *The Wall*, certainly, but the paperback rack in Rader's Drugstore was filled with eyewitness accounts, confessionals, biographies, all with their clustered pages of black-and-white photographs—the entrance gate at Auschwitz, blurry women running naked to the gas chambers in front of laughing Nazis, piles of shoes and hair, a heap of blackened bones pulled out from an oven. All my friends read those books, or at least looked at the photographs, and connected them, I felt, to me. Was it in the blood? The story about my Uncle Herman was confusing—there were different versions. Sometimes my mother said he'd run away to the States to avoid being taken into the Czar's army, which meant an automatic twenty-five-year enlistment; sometimes, she seemed to remember, he'd mutilated himself, cut off his toes, though sometimes the brother she mentioned doing this was David, or sometimes both, so that in my imagination and later, in my stories, as parts of myself, they blended into a single, composite character. I understood in any case that my mother looked upon this action as eminently sensible, if not downright heroic: why put yourself at risk for people who hated your guts and wanted to destroy you? One didn't fight in the interest of any Authority, the lesson seemed to be; one chewed oneself out of the trap and ran.

None of this helped my self-doubts in Bryant Gardens where I was relegated to the position of Jew in war and other games, and where I tied that lesson, that attitude, to those drugstore paperback, movie images of a whole people not even running away, let alone fighting, but walking naked and unresisting to their deaths. Weren't any of our relatives in the resistance? I asked my mother, and for my friends I made up an uncle who'd thrown Molotov cocktails in the Warsaw Ghetto. My fantasy life wrapped itself around slaughter and resistance: I was a victim waiting in line at Auschwitz to be selected, or I was a partisan in a forest, a ghetto fighter, ambushing Nazi patrols. In my daydreams and on the street, and later in a diplomaless high school career full of fights and absences, I went to violence as if it were some test or a chance to disprove the clichés of Jewish cowardice and victimization. I was, in a word, Israel, though not as good at it and without tanks or an air force.

Ironically, or maybe inevitably, the two boyhood fights I remember most vividly were against other Jews. One took place when my mother sent me to Hebrew school in an attempt to Judaize me. For the most part I hated and resented my middle class classmates, kids who came from that softer world of single family homes and college tracks I felt somehow robbed of, kids who seemed to speak a language full of secret meanings and asides I didn't understand, kids who cordially hated me back. One, Howard Hofflink, a large heavy boy who towered over the rest of us, took a particular delight in teasing me about my hoody clothes, my total inappropriateness, until one day I took a swing at him and bloodied his face. When he asked me to meet him after school, I looked at his size and told him sure, but asked him to come to my neighborhood where we could fight undisturbed. To my surprise, he agreed. He was a very big kid but not that smart. Surrounded by a circle of my jeering friends, my best friend Paul Bachmann and I jumped him and wrestled him down. While Paul sat on his legs, I straddled his chest, pinning his arms between my knees, and began driving my fist into his face over and over until something cracked and softened under my knuckles and I felt sick. I looked up and saw that circle of faces staring at me, and I hardened myself and kept driving my fist into Hofflink's big Jewish face until finally someone else said enough, and we moved off in a pack, leaving him unconscious and bleeding. We played football over his supine body until some neighbors chased us away and helped him get out of there. Later, one of the older, tougher kids, clapped me on the back and complimented me on my balls. Some Jew, he said—and I felt at that moment that whatever I'd done to myself to get to that point was worth it.

The second fight was against a boy named Billy Sonders who lived in the neighborhood. He was more independent than I was, sometimes in our crowd, sometimes not, and maybe I resented that or maybe he resented my position in the group: in any case there was always an edge of rivalry between us that had something to do with our Jewishness. One day we were both in the worn little park in the center of the apartment development and words passed and we started to fight. From the beginning it wasn't a pushing, shoving, hoping-someone-will-step-in-and-stop-it boy's kind of fight at all. We punched at each other's faces earnestly and viciously, as if we were trying to obliterate something—grown-up punches, our full weight behind them, looping, from the shoulder rights and lefts. I was bigger and had a longer reach, but Sonders was quicker, and he got in more punches, and neither of us would quit. I wondered long afterwards who it was we were fighting so hard. We fought up and down that park, two cavorting court Jews punching each other for nearly an hour in front of the blank staring windows of the apartment buildings as if in front of an audience that refused to see us, exhausted, our faces swollen and bloody but neither one of us stopping until Billy's uncle came out and cursed me out and Billy told him to stop, it was both of us. Billy, it turned out, went to Vietnam just after I did. He was wounded, I think in the A Shau, strapped onto the back of a tank to be medevacked, and shot another three times while he was on the tank. I saw him just after I got back and we talked a little, but were uneasy with each other—neither of us wanted to talk about the war, and I wonder if we connected it to that fight, as if it had gone on forever, as if Vietnam was the place where it finally took us.

It was in the war, of course, that I'd found the ultimate denial of the stereotype, though at first the Marine Corps, as if determined to reaffirm it, assigned me as a clerk. It was the kind of job people maneuvered to get themselves into; to sabotage it I became the worst clerk I could be. For my sins and to my delight, I was almost immediately reassigned to a perimeter security platoon where I got to sit long, sleepless and sometimes terrifying nights in a miserable monsoon-filled hole in the red Quang Ngai mud, or to wander helmeted and flak-jacketed as if in my own movie, called *Some Jew*, patrolling the scrub jungle, paddies, and thatch-roofed villages around our base camp. Gathering glimpsed images, flashes of a distorted, terrible face whose features I couldn't quite, didn't want to, make out, like the erased faces of the ambushed women and kids in the Polaroid a machine gunner handed me my first week on perimeter as you would hand someone a business card, like no metaphor at all but the place and the thing itself to which my need to live my life as if it was the argument against a preconception had brought me.

So it was, out of a true-believer Kennedy idealism and my own particular desire to prove my willingness and ability to participate in violence—motivations not unlike my country's—that I finally volunteered to extend my tour to be reassigned as a helicopter gunner. And got what I wanted. *Some Jew*. In my twentieth year, twenty years after the end of the Second World War, the son of refugees who'd fled fire and massacre, I found myself in a helicopter, a helmeted figure with a weapon moving over villages where people looked up at me with hate and fear, in a province where, a few years later in my war, hundreds of Vietnamese men, women and children would be herded into ditches and machine-gunned by people who wore the same uniform I wore, an event that surprised me not at all when I first heard about it. It was the face the war had always been rushing to become, the subtext Calley read correctly from the tactics of body count and free fire zones and jellied fire from the sky on farmers' huts, from the answers to our questions: *What do you want? Bodies. How many? Many. Whose? Vietnamese. Which? Vietnamese.*

Eventually the ditches of My Lai would extend in my mind to the ditches of Kolno, a cicatrix just under the skin of the brain.

RUMORS: SEARCH AND DESTROY

There were fiery needle pricks in his foot, jabs felt through a half dream, and he kicked out. His foot connected with something warm and hairy, and he sat up abruptly, sleep sucked away from him like water down a drain. Shit, he said.

He lived in a hootch at Marble Mountain Air Facility with ten others. They had a parachute hung under the ceiling and partitions and shelves made of scrap wood and straw matting.

Up to the month before, the hootch had been a canvas-roofed tent and almost unbearably hot. The new tin roof made it much cooler inside. But now we got rats in here, he said to Rodriguez.

Rats, Sam said, shaking his head. He was lying on his cot, reading a paperback. Jesus Christ. Rats.

Don't let it worry you, Torenelli said.

Eventually it worried all of them.

At least once a night someone would be snapped awake by the feel of a small hot body somewhere in his cot. Usually the rats preferred to attack feet, two naked hunks of meat that tended to become exposed in the night. Sam, for one, could never get back to sleep after feeling a rat. He would begin to drop off, then a mental picture of the animal eating his nose or an eye, jumping across the floor with a chunk of Samface dangling from its mouth, would wake him up. He began to sleep hunched protectively over his genitals, like a man about to fight.

There was a constant squealing at night. It got on the men's nerves, and they would lie awake listening, feeling the sweat from their backs wetting the sandy canvas of their cots. Often they could see the small dimples the rats' feet made as they ran along the top side of the hanging parachute. The men would throw things at the impressions, but the rats were too fast.

It wasn't until Torenelli was killed, actually, that it became an obsession to kill the rats. The night before it happened, he had flipped out at the soft scuffling noises on the silk above his head, and had shot a few holes in the roof with his .45. He would have been court-martialed if he hadn't caught a .50 round that blew most of his chest away, on a medevac the next day.

The rats became a jinx to the men on flight pay after that. They began calling them gooks.

They would lie awake at night, waiting. When someone would feel or hear a rat, he'd yell gook! and Perez would switch on the light. They would chase the creature frantically, upsetting cots, tripping over sea-bags. It would have been a funny Keystone cops scene, except for the hate and fear in the marines' eyes.

At the weekly movie, shown outdoors against a wall of sandbags, they didn't laugh anymore at the little cartoon mice. They would stare at them with hate-rimmed, sleepless eyes and look at the people who did laugh as though they were idiots.

Perez almost got one once. He was chasing it with a Montagnard spear he had picked up near Khe Sanh. He cornered the rat and was trying to jab it with the spear, mock-dueling, laughing hysterically. The animal suddenly reared up on its hind legs and drew back its thin rubber lips, exposing sharp, wicked-looking teeth. Its eyes bulged with frantic hate. Perez was taken aback and stopped jabbing for a split second. The rat immediately leapt away and disappeared into some unseen hole.

On the day the hunt was finally successful they killed eleven rats. It happened right after Perez and Billings were knocked out of the air while on a resupply to Hill 327. A recoilless rifle round had punched a huge hole in the side of their helicopter, but they were able to autorotate down with no one hurt.

They all sat around that night telling sea stories about getting shot down. Perez was grateful the round hadn't exploded the gas tank. Thank fuck it didn't explode, he said. All it had meant was a little time with the grunts for his gunner, Billings, and him. He was shaking his head when they all heard the squeal, punctuating his prayer. Gook! Perez yelled, his face hard.

The slick brown body jumped across the room, and they flew after it, yelling. They were surprised to trap the rat almost immediately. It stood on its hind legs in an inescapable corner, squealing shrilly.

Sam was the first to see why the rat was so easily trapped. He heard a soft noise from the opposite corner of the hut and went to look. Billings saw him move and followed. Damn, he yelled, fervently, triumphantly, it's got babies! It was trying to lead us away.

There were ten of them, blind and pink, clutching at each other with small groping hands.

Billings took a long piece of copper wire and, kneeling, stuck its end through each baby's small, pulsing throat. The tinny sound of their squealing gradually died as the wire tore through flesh, until only the squeal of the trapped mother could be heard.

Billings whooped and brandished the chain of dead babies in front of the mother, Then he took them outside and plunged their still twitching mass into the large water barrel just outside the hut. His face was alight and strained.

Donner, the big silent boy from Kansas, clubbed at the mother. She kept up her high-pitched squealing, her eyes darting towards the water barrel outside. Perez grabbed a canvas sack and dropped it over the stunned rat. The rest of the men stood around him, watching. He picked the sack up and carried it outside to the barrel, then took it by the bottom and shook the mother out into the water. The two ends of the wire on which the babies were dangling had caught on the rim of the barrel, and the bodies just broke the water, next to her face. She was still alive, swimming frantically.

Perez began pushing her face under with a piece of wood. He kept holding her down for longer and longer periods, but each time he let up she would still be alive and struggling. He swore at her.

Donner went into the hut and came back with his can of deodorant. He waited until Perez let the rat's head break the water, then sprayed the deodorant through the flame of his cigarette lighter. It sent out a sheet of flame: a miniature flame thrower. The hair on her face began to burn off, leaving her with surprisingly pink skin that soon blackened and began peeling off like singed paper. Her eyes changed from alive black berries to small dead ones and then to cinders. They could almost see her blood boil. She kept coming up alive.

Perez and Donner began to look panicky. Die, goddamn you, Perez swore, under his breath. The rest of the men watched silently. Both Perez and Donner were sweating profusely. They held the rat under for impossibly long periods, but she kept surfacing, her burned face coming up next to her dead babies, her mouth opening and closing, grabbing lungfuls of air and fire.

After a long time, she died.

Perez and Donner stood there for a while looking at her gently bobbing body. Their mouths were hanging open and they looked drained and exhausted. Everybody else went silently back into the hootch.

THE PORCH

"But other mountains lack the ambiance of Vermont's."
—a Bread Loaf coordinator

"People come and go, taking prozac on the lawn."
—Meir Wigoder

I went to Poland after spending two weeks in Boston. Who I was with and what I did there became another subtext for the trip in a way I should explain. I'd just had a novel come out, then and though it disappeared almost immediately and was only the second book I'd written with a Vietnam theme, a number of the reviews it had received categorized me as a "Vietnam writer." Fair enough, I thought, but also somewhat dismissive and inaccurate—none of my novels were actually set in the war, and I'd also lived for years in Israel and had written two novels out of that experience. But the reviews, the thinking I was going through about my writing, made me a little hesitant about going back to Boston, where I'd been meeting each summer with a group of writers whose commonality was the war. We were all, I think, a little leery, or felt we should be leery, of attending conferences which categorized us and our work only through that background, as if that year or so we had spent in Vietnam made us, black or white, into a new race or gender.

Maybe in some ways it had. "Vietnam," Michael Herr wrote, "was what we had instead of a happy childhood." Maybe the war was the prism through which we'd come to regard and judge the world. Why not? In doing that, in our country, we hardly seemed to be alone.

To be truthful, I was looking forward to seeing the other Vietnam writers again. The William Joiner Center for the Study of War and Social Consequences at UMass Boston had been holding the summer conference, a series of readings, writing workshops and symposia about war and the writing of it, for about six years. Many of the writers whose work had in one way or another centered around the Vietnam war, some well known, others (my category) known mostly to each other, turned up at Joiner: one grenade in the middle of this group, we felt, and America could forget the war all it wanted. Most of us lived together for the two weeks, sharing quarters with the director, Kevin Bowen a Vietnam veteran poet and his wife Leslie and his kids and his neighbors, the Davidsons, on a nicely tree-shaded street of large old duplex houses in unfashionable Dorchester, a working class neighborhood in Boston that had given a disproportionate share of kids to the war and which had now become a refugee center, its main street, Dorchester Avenue, described by a Boston Irish city council member, caught *in flagrante video*, as looking "like fucking Saigon."

Three of us, the novelist Larry Heinemann, the poet Bruce Weigl and I had been coming back each year to teach writing workshops and do readings. We tended to feel comfortable with each other, as did most of the veteran writers—there weren't the ego competitions and pecking-order fights Heinemann and Weigl had experienced at other writers' conferences, and anyway it always felt good to relax into our true shapes, away from the normals. "I love this place," the San Francisco poet George Evans, who had come for the first time that summer, told me. He had stopped going to writing conferences after getting a scholarship to Bread Loaf some years before. When the conference coordinator who met him had asked about his trip—he'd come up from Pennsylvania through the Alleghenies—he'd begun describing the beauty of the mountains he'd hitched through. "Yes, yes," she said impatiently, "but other mountains lack the ambiance of Vermont's."

I'm not sure what to call what we had at Joiner. Meir Wigoder, an Israeli friend who visited that year said he saw some core in me he'd never seen before. "But you guys are not," he wrote me later, "simply living again what you once lived—it's not nostalgia, not a meeting of friends from a platoon who speak of how they fucked those gooks, but a continuous need to understand what you did before when you did not understand." He was right and less than right. So much of our writing lives had been involved with war and consequences, and sometimes it was as if the sleepless nights and the drinking and talking of the talk and the readings were all muttered evocations, cabalistic rituals, so that the memories we evoked in each other would rise and mingle with characters from our fiction and poetry like transparencies sliding over our lives, what we joined to at Joiner. After classes or readings, we would sit on the Bowen/Davidson porch in Dorchester and drink and talk far into the night, the wind chimes that hung above the porch railing a soft toll under our murmur, as insistent as the staccato of shots coming to us from the gang drive-bys up the street. Weigl was busy composing a textbook to teach poetry to the dead ("Chapter One: you look like a god. Don't just sit there. Write something.") He wrote poetry for the living that pinned the heart, and I'd see him teaching his workshop students with the kind of gentleness that seems exquisite as a shiver in the nerves when you see it in a large and turbulent man. When he'd come back to the house, in the afternoons, he'd change and then go out and start sinking baskets into the hoop on the garage behind the house, competing hard against himself and then competing aggressively in pick-up games against the black neighborhood teenagers who would come over, as if he needed to do something with whatever was re-forming under all that nice. The games would leave him blanched and breathless, his face drained. He was a big man, a steelworker's kid who played high school football in the mean steel town of Lorain, Ohio before ending up in the First Air Cavalry, and he still lifted weights. But like all of us he was in his forties, and I'd look at him with real concern when he came off the court, though a good part of the concern was selfish, was for myself and what I saw forming again in myself.

Heinemann was the best known of us, a National Book Award winner for his novel *Paco's Story*, though that evening, two summers before, he'd read from his new book, *Cooler By The Lake*, a comic novel about Chicago which he introduced by describing as a book where nobody died and everybody got what he wanted, and which I saw, therefore, as still a novel about Vietnam, a literary equivalent of the Gulf War. Listening to him though, I'd found I missed Paco: Paco with his whole wiped out platoon of ghosts riding around in his head, commenting on the world like a seared Greek chorus. We're all Paco at Joiner, I thought. I hadn't been sure what to read—I'd brought a number of things, but at the last minute I decided to read a chapter from my new novel about a Bangkok bar full of drunken, nostalgic vets, Fat Al and Chuckie's-in-Love and Helicopter Harry in Bangkok, hell as a never ending R&R, a vision inspired by Joiner. "Sound good to me," Fat Al belched. "Sure thing, Helicopter Harry." Chuckie's-in-Love raised his face. "Tell him about raping the hootch and burning the peasant," he said...

We went drinking after the reading, finally settling in at a bar at the edge of the Combat Zone. When we left at closing time, the city had changed, the people gone and the buildings half-erased by mist and we were moving in that displaced edged out state when you're half-drunk and sleepless and still high from the reading and the dark, trash-blown streets you need to pass are deserted except for the dealers and whores on the corners, eyeballing. "The hell we doing?" Heinemann muttered, but we followed Weigl like a point man, into the Zone. At the T station on the Common, rows of silent Chinese men stood five or six deep before each pay phone; they turned in unison to stare at us, their eyes socketed in black shadows, their faces bleached by the streetlights. "Come on," Heinemann said. "We can still get the last train to Dorchester."

We went downstairs. There was no one else there except a night crew of hardhats working in a flickering wizard's circle around a masked man with an acetylene torch. The last train pulled up and stopped in front of us, and its doors slid apart abruptly and loudly in the empty station. All the seats to the left of the door were occupied by Haitians talking softly to each other in Creole. They looked at us and fell silent, drawing together. A skinny white man sat by himself at the other end of the car, long dank hair falling over a narrow pocked face, a black rectangular box at his feet. I saw Weigl staring and I knew what he was seeing: the subway of the dead scene in *Jacob's Ladder*, when the film's hero, back from Vietnam, sees the blankly staring faces of demons in subway windows. It was his favorite movie.

Heinemann sat quietly, looking at Weigl, shaking his head.

"Wiggle," he said.

Weigl sat next to me. I asked him where Gloria Emerson, a writer who had come with us, had gone after the reading.

"You know Gloria," he said.

The skeletal white man suddenly rose and glared at him. He shambled over to us. "I may not know Gloria," he said. "But." He opened the black box and pulled out a banjo. "But I do know Lola."

Lalalala Lola

Lalalala Lola

We're on the Ladder now, Weigl grinned at me.

The train stopped and the door opened and Fat Al and Chuckie's-in-Love stepped through it into the world, both unshaven and staggering, one thin and hawkish in a stained black raincoat, the other dark-jowled, foul-smelling. The fat man glared around the car, burped, stared straight at Weigl and me.

"When I was in the Nam," he bellowed to the car.

Weigl smiled at me, his face damaged in the harsh light.

The man looked at him blearily.

"You saying you were in Vietnam?" Weigl asked.

"Bruce," Heinemann said.

Fat Al knit his forehead, belched as if that was the thought he'd drawn from it. "What the fuck all you know about it?"

"Just wondering, bro. I was there with the First Cav."

"Bullshit. You never were."

"Bruce," Heinemann said. Weigl grinned.

"Bullshit?" he said.

"Let's all," Heinemann said, "get home alive."

I looked at the two of them, Weigl and Heinemann, Heinemann mostly sober, acting his age. It suddenly seemed like a choice. We're all Paco at Joiner. The thought snagged in my mind, the music. We're Paco at Joiner

Lalalala Lola

Lalalala Lola

Chuckie's-in-Love was tugging at Fat Al's arm. "Hey man," he said, very carefully, "we got to get off at Savin Hill. Otherwise we miss our last connection."

"Ain't life grand," Fat Al said.

"Who were you with?" I asked him. "In Vietnam?"

He glared at me. "Marines," he said, and laughed, surprised at his own history.

"Where were you?"

"Where the fuck was I? Where the fuck were you?"

The Haitians had fallen silent and were stirring uneasily. Where the fuck was I?

Lalalala Lola

Lalalala Lola

"Yes," Weigl said. "Sure, a little head banging. I don't mind."

"My Lai," the drunk sneered. "I was at My Lai."

"Bullshit," I said. "There were no marines at My Lai," I said, feeling a sharp rise of rage, that he was only able to call up those two words to mean the war, that he'd leaked off my pages, that he wouldn't leave me the fuck alone.

He glared at me. "What'd you say?"

"I don't think you were there. At all."

I saw Heinemann looking at me in disgust.

The train stopped. "Hey," Chuckie's-in-Love asked, looking nervously at Bruce's size. "This Savin Hill?"

"Absolutely," Heinemann said. The stop was UMass. "Hurry up," Heinemann said. "You'll miss your connection."

"Right," Chuckie's-in-Love said. He pushed his friend out of the door. Fat Al stood uncertainly on the platform, still glaring. The doors closed, severing him from me.

You who return to me as vines in the deep night under fog, wrote George Evans. Everything we'd thought of in ourselves as past or relegated safely into the characters and situations of fiction and poetry was still there, and it barged into our nights, and we sat with it on the porch, and it occurred to me that while all of this seemed to be producing art, I couldn't see that it was doing us as individuals much good. Behind our eyes, each of us, was a shimmer of death; like doofus oracles, we made shapes out of it to produce what we produced; it was the coin of our reputations; it was how we made our living. Maybe we were vultures.

So what? As long as our writing had some sort of redemptive, preemptive value, it was necessary, whatever other prices and compensations went along with it, right? Besides, if not us, then who? We shared the war like a childhood. We spoke the same language. We shared the same fear that no one else understood it. That the war was being rewritten in order to present the country with what it wanted to hear about itself: it had engaged in a defined and noble mission against an evil inhuman enemy. I'd read how Tom Clancy and Tom Selleck had become good buddies, writer and actor, print and screen; they twined in my mind and nightmares into a leering Janus figurehead for the Age of Convenient Illusion: neither of them in the war, both shaping it to fit a picture in their minds as unchallenged by experience as the rest of the country: America as Jack Ryan and Thomas Magnum, the Vietnamese as cruel inhuman slime. The country outside the porch on which we sat seemed entangled in a conspiracy to make up stories that would make itself feel better, the never was's and wannabes selling the country the myths it wanted out of the war, rewriting it to order, the usual. Making up the lies that lies come from. Who the hell could compete with that depth of wishful thinking? The lesson of the war seemed to be that everything was whatever you wanted it to be. It was the attitude that had allowed the war in the first place.

After everything that had gone down, who needed that kind of shitty irony?

You who return to me as vines in the deep night under fog,
have come at a bad time, a time when the world is obsessed
with rubbing you smooth, and its concentration
on ceremony brings you to nothing...

Sometimes, often, I felt I was standing behind a thick glass screen, pushing my face and hands against it, calling out something nobody on the other side could hear. It wasn't a dissimilar state to the way I'd felt just after the war when I'd gone to a peace demonstration: as if I was moving through the hundreds of thousands of chanting people like a ghost. Maybe Weigl had something. Maybe that was our Writing Conference Theme. Writing to the Dead. The Writer as the Dead. You look like a God. Shut up. Maybe we were the way I remembered the veterans at that demonstration, nice to have around the Halls of Literature as tokens of moral legitimacy, but don't get too close. Maybe we were one-shot idiots savant, our appeal rooted in the too-easy, the facile crucible, the exaggerated drama of war, an attitude clarified and epitomized for me in a review by Ted Solotaroff.

Before coming to Boston, I'd read Thom Jones' *The Pugilist At Rest* and thought that here was someone doing what Hemingway did at his best, meditating on the necessary attempts and the failures to find graceful ways to move through and ultimately reject a world of murder and brutality. But one wasn't to speak of Hemingway any more. A few months later, Solotaroff, writing in *The Nation*, maintained that Jones was too talented to keep writing stories about soldiers and boxers, "angry people and their power trips," about men and women struggling to find rules of behavior in a violent and brutal world. "Most serious matters are closed to the hard-boiled," he paraphrased Saul Bellow, and suggested that Jones' editor steer him to writing stories about "tangled family distress" instead. A number of questions occurred to me. Was the serious twentieth century writer to pretend that atrocity wasn't central to the experience of our time? Did Solotaroff and I live in the same twentieth century? Did he ever ride the T? Why did the mountains of Vermont have a special ambiance? Would being machine gunned into a ditch be considered a case of tangled family distress? Should the serious twentieth century writer disappear up his own anus?

Something for your poetry, no? whispered Carolyn Forché's Salvadorean Colonel, bringing his jar of human ears to the porch, setting them on the table—she'd come up to be with us, her tickets of admission a first husband who had brought only his body back from Vietnam and her own memories of the war she'd seen in El Salvador. Lately she had taken to carrying a copy of a *New York Times* article about the massacres around with her, to show people who were sure the ears were only a metaphor. *What you have heard is true*, the poem insists, and the Colonel spills the severed ears out and some lie on the floor as if pressed to hear human voices. Poetry for the dead. As if we'd been drawn in our writing into an end of the century Talmudic dialogue between

ourselves and the insistent dead, like the dialogue
Heinemann's Paco carries on in his head with *his*
platoon of ghosts. "But that's the way of the world, or so
the fairy tales go," the ghosts warn Paco. "The people
with the purse strings and apron strings gripped in their
hot and soft little hands denounce war stories—with
perfect diction and practiced gestures—as a geek-
monster species of evil-ugly rumor."

> *But the lie swings back again,* wrote Weigl
> *the lie works only as long as it takes to speak*
> *and the girl runs only as far*
> *as the napalm allows*
> *until her burning tendons and crackling*
> *muscles draw her up*
> *into that final position*
> *burning bodies so perfectly assume. Nothing*
> *can change that, she is burned behind my eyes*
> *and not your good love and not the rain-swept air*
> *and not the jungle-green*
> *pasture unfolding before us can deny it.*

Two summers before, I'd sat with him and
Heinemann and Gloria Emerson, a writer and former
correspondent who had seen more war than any of us.
It was a warm evening and troops had just started being
sent to Saudi Arabia, and a new war had begun, a war, it
seemed clear to us, that whatever its stated political,
strategic or even moral purpose was, in the end, the
country's most ambitious attempt to revise our

confusing war to a better, happier ending—as if Selleck, or Clancy, the frustrated 4-F warrior with the tank his wife had given him for his birthday sitting on his lawn, or Stallone, the Swiss girls' school vet, or Schwartzenegger, the future HumVee driver had all finally gotten to write one of their own. It was the national Entertainment. We watched spotlights from some Dorchester shopping center play against the clouds, a miniature image of the light show that we'd all see over Baghdad the next January, though we didn't make the connection then. What we did then was convince ourselves they were UFO's. We wanted aliens in the world. They would keep us company. They would hover above the bullshit. They would have a true record.

RUMORS: MORATORIUM

Mor*a*to*ri*um, n. 1. an authorization to delay
payment due

Deborah asked, Everything all right?

Just the early morning broods.

She watched his hands as he soaped them.

I'm still scared of how you're taking it.

How am I taking it?

Too seriously. Like some momentous, ceremonial
occasion. But it's just a party to most of the people.
That's why I stopped going.

I thought you stopped going because of me.

That's what I mean.

They sat down on the bed, settling back against the
pillow. She put her head on his chest.

In our Operations tent, he said, there was this
gunny sergeant; he kept a framed photograph on his
desk. Not the wife and kids, but this picture from the
New York Times, a shot of one of the first demon-
strations. He'd circled one marcher's head with a grease
pencil he used on the flight status board to write in the

names of the crews going on missions. Above the guy's head he wrote, "Traitor—to be killed." The circle was real thick and dark, and you could see he'd pressed down very hard with rage because of the smudge where the tip of the pencil had broken off.

Nobody's going to draw a halo around your head, Deborah said.

He got off the bed and walked over to the closet. The night before, he'd hung up his jungle shirt and some jeans and hooked the hanger over the door, ready as if he were going on an early morning flight, a mission. He'd pinned his silver aircrew wings to the shirt. The gunny, he remembered suddenly, was the kind of NCO who would write people up for chickenshit, stateside offenses like being out of uniform, as if he felt he had a mission to maintain standards, standards that didn't apply in the circumstances of the war.

He put on the shirt, running his fingertips over the metal wings. A knock startled him. He waited until Deborah had pulled on a long shirt and then he opened the door.

Barry was wearing a khaki shirt with his ribbons and Combat Infantry Badge on it. He grinned: their choice of clothing hadn't been planned.

Green side out, he said. How you feeling?

Traitor—to be killed.

Absolutely.

They made a pit stop at Maryland House. The two men had a smoke while they waited for Deborah and Barry's girl Phyllis to get out of the rest room. He had another while Barry pumped the gas. A silver-gray Plymouth pulled up next to them. In the passenger seat was a blond woman with a beehive hairdo. She glanced at him, then patted her hair, as if his gaze had made her conscious of it. The driver was wearing a khaki uniform, Army class A's, like Barry's, a colored rectangle of ribbons on his chest. The woman tilted the mirror again and a rhomboid of light projected over the face of the soldier inside. The face looked vaguely accusing and pissed-off. He'd been holding a kind of tension, he realized, since the day before, since he'd decided to go to the demonstration. Now something in the angle of light, in the blurred features of the face, allowed that tension to relax in a kind of internal collapse into the face of Jim Hardesty.

Hardesty was a boy who had died in his place, flying gunner on a routine resupply mission to Hill 327 during what was to have been the last week of the war for both of them. The squadron was rotating to Okinawa to get new helicopters; it had lost five aircraft and the remaining ships were in bad shape after four solid months of operations along the DMZ. He and Jim Hardesty were in the last increment to leave. On nearly the last day he had drawn flight duty, but Hardesty had asked if he could take it instead. He couldn't even remember the reason for it, he didn't know Hardesty that well; they weren't really friends, just military acquaintances. Maybe Hardesty figured he'd be called to fly the next day anyway and wanted to get it over with;

maybe he needed a mission for an air medal. There were enough stories of people killed in the last days of their tours. Outside the war, you told stories like that to prevent them from happening to you. But, in the war, telling them was more like calling something to life. If Hardesty wanted to take his place, that was fine with him. They'd gone to the operations sergeant, the one with the photograph on his desk, and made the switch. That night the helicopter in which he would have flown gunner went on a standard resupply flight to a company of grunts. It was on approach when it came under fire, and a single bullet hit the helicopter and penetrated it and Hardesty's body, going through the gunner's seat where he would have been sitting, entering below the bottom edge of Hardesty's flak jacket instead of his, traveling perpendicularly through Hardesty's body instead of his.

Now he stood alive in a gas station in Maryland watching the face of a soldier watching him from behind a windshield.

He wondered if the request to switch had been a last minute effort on Hardesty's part to deal with some perceived internal weakness while he still had the chance. There were people who came to the war for that. Perhaps many people. He remembered how scared Hardesty had been. In the old aviator's canard, he wasn't afraid of flying, only of coming down. The country itself filled Hardesty with terror; it was so unlike the flat Kansas plains he came from. It pulsed with the over-lush greens of an evil Oz. The fragmented mirrors of its paddies held images of broken helicopters in their depths. Its jagged, broody cordilleras and secretive triple-canopied jungle randomly and maliciously spat fire upwards. The helicopters would only touch the land briefly to release men onto it, then touch briefly again soon after to pick up the bodies of the same men, torn as if they had been gnawed by the country. What happened in the time between was unknown to the helicopter crews. Hardesty had told him how his finger had started to tremble on the trigger even in cold L.Z.'s as if on some hair trigger inside himself that was wearing closer and closer to the sear. He'd understood Hardesty; he was worn in the same places; he sat in the same seat; he knew the feeling of helplessness. On missions, the gunner was an impotent spectator except when shooting his gun. His helicopter had flown cover on one insert when Hardesty's helicopter had let off a squad of grunts and the crews had watched in horror, not frozen, but hovering, darting, hosing the treeline with fire, but all of it useless as the grunts ran in fire-team rushes toward that treeline, falling, one fire team after another cut down, and not one hesitating, just working, moving professionally toward the trees that were killing them; one man after another zigging and zagging and falling as if it were some well rehearsed, tactically planned process they were all following to get killed quickly. Then on Hardesty's next flight, his helicopter developed a hydraulic leak and had to autorotate down to a hard landing in a paddy, the ship spinning, the land sucking him down to itself. A clearly pregnant woman squatted among the rice shoots, watching him come into her life. She'd frozen, war-wise, knowing that the helicopters shot anyone who ran, not knowing that Hardesty was in this one. That night he'd joked about getting two gooks with one round. The phrase became a standard with the air crews, a measure of shooting proficiency. A joke.

The face behind the windshield mouthed silently at him. He saw the woman put a hand on the soldier's shoulder, as if restraining him.

The memories were coming faster, some compressed spring he'd lived with so long its tightness had become normal suddenly released in his mind. He remembered how he'd flown back to Travis Air Force Base in San Francisco on the same C-130 with about twenty other men from his squadron whose tours had finished while they were on Okinawa. It was the nearest thing the war had to the traditional coming back as a unit: the random mathematics of their time in country giving them an accidental parade, even if it only consisted of being herded up the ramp of the cargo plane together. For the first time they wore the class A khaki uniforms they hadn't seen for over a year, whitened crease lines on them where the cloth had been folded in their stored sea-bags, new ribbons and silver combat aircrew wings bright on their chests. Perhaps noticing the wings, some of the Air Force crew brought them coffee; they had wings too; they were all birdmen, brothers of the air. How was it, the airmen had asked, and the marines told them sea stories, air stories, shot down stories, shoot up the village stories, toss the prisoners stories. He told how Hardesty had gotten two gooks with one round. But the airmen didn't laugh. They didn't get the joke. They looked at the marines, at the wings on their chests, strangely. Then the marines fell silent, too. They blinked as if awakening from a dream in which the laws and customs of the world had been suspended. He could feel a silence folding around them and he knew that they, he, wouldn't talk about the war anymore, or if they did, they'd try to fit it into more expected and acceptable references. That nobody would get the joke.

What are you men doing?

He saw that the soldier had gotten out of the Plymouth. Focusing back, he realized that he hadn't even noticed the process; it played in his mind like a memory behind the memories of that flight home and Hardesty: the car door opening, the frowning face, the woman tugging the soldier's arm, trying to pull him back. There were silver first lieutenant's bars on the man's collar. His eyes went automatically to the ribbons. The yellow and red Vietnam service ribbon was there, but there were no CIB, no wings, no purple heart, only the been-there ribbons.

I said what are you men doing? The lieutenant frowned at them.

You men? Barry said, squinting at him.

The lieutenant's face went red. Let me see your i.d.'s.

Barry laughed. Look, L.T., we're not in the service anymore.

Then you have no right to be wearing those uniforms. There's a law against impersonating a soldier. He glared at them. I know where you're going. You're both disgraces. I want your names—both of you.

Barry looked, startled, at the lieutenant, then began laughing. You want to write me up, he said in wonder. The lieutenant stared at him, still frowning. You want to write me up now. He laughed more. Hey, lieutenant, where the fuck were you? Out of the corner of his eye, he saw Phyllis and Deborah coming back from the ladies' room. Why don't you just di-di the fuck out of here, he said. You understand that term, lieutenant? Or you just impersonating a dick head?

He saw Barry pull the nozzle out of the gas tank and screw on the cap, his shoulders stiff and high, his face tight. Barry spun around, arcing the gas nozzle close to the lieutenant's face. Some gas globbed from the end and the lieutenant stepped back slightly. Barry nodded and poked the nozzle forward, closer, and the lieutenant backed up. Gas dribbled onto his spit shine. Barry held his lit cigarette in his other hand, between thumb and forefinger. He flicked it. Ever see a gook flambé, L.T., a crispy critter? he asked. Ever write one up? No? Where were you when that was going down? Like the man asked—where the fuck were you? Some office? Pointing your pointer at some map overlay, some grid I was on? Want a ciggie? Souvenir you Salem? Want a light? No? Then like my friend said, you better di-di. Don't let your alligator mouth overload your lizard ass and all that other kind of Vietnam talk.

The lieutenant stared at him. You men will hear about this, I promise you. I have your license number.

The woman in the Plymouth stuck her head out of the window. Leave them alone, Martin. We're late.

You're late, Martin, he said, coming up next to Barry. Move on, lieutenant pogue. You got my number—give me a call sometimes.

The lieutenant left. He turned around. Deborah and Phyllis were staring at him and Barry in the same way Deborah had stared at his hands that morning.

The movement of the march trembled between the buildings. He felt an answering shudder in his chest. He couldn't see either end of the column. On the car radio they'd heard there were half a million people in the streets of Washington. The announcer had commented that this was the equivalent of the number of troops still in Vietnam. Similar numbers were reported from New York, San Francisco, Chicago.

He tried to hang onto a feeling of purposefulness in being part of the movement of so many people. But instead he found himself settling into the dullness he always assumed when marching in a column, an interior blankness that he moved in until he got where he was going. The people around him were linking arms, smiling at each other, chanting for peace now. He lip-synched the words, feeling self-conscious. Deborah had been pushed a little ways from him, and a woman hooked her arm with his and grinned at him. Her other arm was linked with a priest's. The priest smiled at him too. He saw the priest's gaze brush the wings on his chest, the man catching his eye, nodding in approval. Brothers of the air. He brought his hand up, covered the insignia. He had the wings, he needed the halo. I'm out of uniform, priest. Write me up. The chanting grew louder. Phyllis, Barry's arm draped over her shoulder, looked around at him. She was smiling, too. I can't hear you, she mouthed. All of a sudden he was back in boot camp. Get back and do it again. Get it right this time. I can't hear you. All the people around him were chanting and grinning as if they knew something about it, moving their signs and banners up and down in a cadence. They didn't know, but they'd been told. I can't hear you! he yelled. He thought how they would look without the noise coming from their mouths, the way he would turn down the sound on the TV and watch the grotesque pantomimes of the news announcers, their inane smiles encompassing images of corpses and shooting men and burning hootches. When he'd first gotten back, before he met Deborah, he'd rented a small room and spent hours watching TV, as if he could plug himself back into the country, get back on some wavelength he was missing. On the screen, little gray figures ran across paddies, fell, rose; he was one of them, escaped right out of the box, loose in the streets. Out of uniform. Impersonating a human being. PEACE NOW! he yelled, and laughed. The woman and the priest laughed too, but he laughed louder, until they looked at him uneasily. He could get the two of them with one round. They were all bunched up with someplace to go.

He couldn't see Deborah. Suddenly a truck pulled in front of him from a side street, breaking into the crowd. It was draped with VC and North Vietnamese flags and there was a rock band on its bed, playing very hard, the marching band for this parade. The music jerked the crowd. He could see one of the player's faces very clearly. It was pale and pimpled and the boy's eyes were blank as if all his emotions had been poured into the blurred motion of his fingers on the guitar strings. The boy had made a VC flag into a vest, was bare-chested under it, his upper body white and skinny. He stared at the boy's face. He wanted to break it with his fist, knead expressions into it, give it to Jim Hardesty. But the face stayed blank. His feelings didn't particularly move it.

Hey, man, he yelled at the boy. Hey, you're out of uniform. The boy cupped one hand behind his ear and smiled helplessly. He didn't get the joke.

He looked away from the boy, searching for Deborah; she'd been squeezed a little further forward. He spotted Barry and Phyllis near her. They were looking up at the spectators in the windows of government office buildings, searching for anyone cheering them from behind the walls of legitimate authority. Some of the windows had jungly green plants behind them, as if screening another world that hid behind the facade of the building. Faces peered at him in silent disapproval. They had his number. The lieutenant's face mouthed angrily at him from behind the glass. It blurred and disappeared.

Move on, lieutenant pogue.

He'd stopped to look up at the windows, letting the crowd break around him. When he looked back down, he couldn't see Deborah anywhere. He felt a sense of trapped panic. He began shoving through the marchers. The crowd was a pressure at his temples. He pushed through, feeling bodies like vines and roots, holding his passage for an instant, then giving way and slipping past him. He grasped with his hands in a swimming motion, taking people by the shoulders and parting them out of his way. They glared at him, but said nothing until he was past; then they'd start chanting again as if he'd never touched them. Over here! he heard Deborah yell. She was next to the priest. He made a final thrust and broke through, reaching out blindly, connecting with the priest's arm. He gripped it. All those personnel wishing halos will assemble to the right and rear of the duty priest. Semper fi, sky pilot, you got yours, how'm I doing? The priest was staring at him. He released his arm.

You're late, sky pilot, he thought. Move on. Don't let your alligator intentions overload your lizard dimensions.

They were moving now through a gap in a row of parked school buses and into the Mall area. As the column broke and spread into the clearing, he could see for the first time the vastness of the crowd. It filled the center of the city, the white tower of the monument rising from its center. Half a million people, Deborah said into his ear, half a million was his number and he could see it unabstract, solidly filling space. He could see with his eyes what half a million was. He felt utterly outside them, on the other side of a hard, transparent screen. The half million were laughing and dancing and he tried to think about Jim Hardesty who'd died in his place and the woman and the future Hardesty had killed from his place and in their name, these people around him who wouldn't look at him, and he looked at them and he could see how they would be dead, all dead and lying on the grass, silent and spilling into the earth. I can't hear you, he thought. He sat down where he was. He was waiting for something inside himself and when it finally came and he began crying, it came in waves so hard he felt they had to move out of him, ripple through the hugeness of the crowd. But when he looked up, he only saw a woman staring as if surprised at what he was doing. He couldn't stop it. There was no release in it. Deborah put a hand on his shoulder. He bowed his head back down, pressing his face against the cloth of his shirt and the noise faded again. It was as if he were alone in the cradle of his arms.

AS IF FROM LEAVES,
AS IF FROM SKY

Bruce Weigl, Larry Heinemann and Kevin Bowen had been back to Vietnam on a trip that I'd been invited to but didn't attend. Of the Joiner writers that summer, Tim O'Brien and Bob Mason had also been invited and also didn't go. Our reasons, I suspect, may have been similar—something to do with other plans and commitments and something to do with a reluctance to confront a place which we had relegated to fiction and imagination. I wanted it to stay there. I had no sense of nostalgia about the war. I didn't particularly want to visit old base camps and battlefields, to confront the dead; I felt no particular need for some sort of geographic closure; I was a little afraid of it. What I felt was something of the same reluctance, in fact, I would feel about going to Poland.

Now the four of us were going to Logan airport to meet three writers from Vietnam: two men—Nguyen Quang Thieu and Huu Thinh, and a woman, Le Minh Khue.

Thieu was a younger writer, in his thirties, but the other two were veterans of the American war. They had been invited by Joiner, through the Vietnam Writers' Union in Hanoi, to meet with American writers, veterans of what the Americans called the Vietnam war.

It was difficult to find parking at Logan, and we had to walk a distance to the terminal, going through underground garages and over traffic bridges and through connecting tunnels. As we walked, I started wondering what all this would look like to the Vietnamese, how it would be for them to come to this country, a place which even during the war, even when and because they had been locked with us in a death grip, must have attached to complex and contradictory visions in their thoughts and imaginations—as it was in ours. Heinemann told me that Le Minh Khue had mentioned to him that she'd carried books by Jack London and Hemingway in her rucksack the whole time she was a sapper doing bomb disposal on the Ho Chi Minh Trail. She'd learned, she said, about both survival and death from those writers, lessons that I imagined other Americans had helped her with as well.

The terminal was crowded and we couldn't get past security to go to the gate where the plane would land. Weigl and I went to the counter to see if we could get permission: when we gave her the names of the writers, the clerk said she could give passes to just two of us. For a second I thought about giving my pass to Bowen or Heinemann, who after all knew these people. But I wanted to see their first reactions. So I didn't.

When he was a soldier, Weigl had told me, when the other soldiers were eating C-rats, he would eat Vietnamese food with the ARVN: he had been one of those G.I.'s who had loved the country even during the war: its landscape, its Otherness. His trips to Vietnam since had been watersheds for him; he'd fallen in love with the country again—not with the south, with the places of the war, but with Hanoi, with the whole land that had been withheld from us by the war and by what we were doing there. He was excited to see the Vietnamese again.

We watched the small two-engine commuter plane land—the writers had had to transfer at Kennedy. The hatch opened and an Asian man emerged and came down the steps. I looked at Weigl. "Nope," he said. Another Asian man came out, and an Asian woman, another, anther Asian man, more, as if the plane had come directly from the far East. Weigl started to look nervous. Then he smiled. A stocky dark-complexioned man with a wispy mustache stood at the top of the mobile stairway, reflecting Weigl's grin back at him. Waving at us, he came down and stood on the tarmac and then he raised his hands above his head, looking around at America and flashing V for victory signs. "Thieu," Weigl said.

The other two Vietnamese were smiling at us also. The head of the delegation, the poet Huu Thinh, was a slim, very handsome man in his fifties, who laughed in delight to see Weigl. The other writer, Le Minh Khue, was a slight woman with a lovely haunted face. She was

a short-story writer and novelist who had spent her
youth on the Ho Chi Minh Trail under American
bombs, one of that quiet army of women that every
night erased the damage we'd done as if we'd never
touched the place. Her greeting was less effusive; she
smiled warmly but there was a reserved sadness in her
eyes. As I took Le Minh Khue's bag—it was surprisingly
light for the only bag she'd brought—I found that I was
trying to see my country through her eyes during her
first step out of the airlock: the large, strangely smiling
Americans in front of pictures of other large smiling
Americans on the advertisements lining the corridors,
the science-fiction maze of windowed tunnels and
traffic bridges, a glimpse of Boston's skyline framed by
the buildings of the airport, the descent into the
stairwells and levels of the multilevel parking garage and
then out into the hot, bright air, a shimmering sense of
clumsy energy and power that edged into an impossible
collage: Robert Jordan lying on pine needles, the lined
weather-beaten faces of men in furs crouched by
flickering campfires in a vast white silence that melted
into the scream of jets and the rain of silver crystals
burning down through the canopy, the roar and flash of
bombs, the earth she'd smoothed back over the scars in
her country with her hands. The Trail she'd stepped
onto when she was fifteen that had brought her, finally,
here.

I wondered what she saw when she looked at my
face.

The Vietnamese had each brought one small carry-on suitcase and when we got back to Dorchester, they opened them and began handing out gifts to us. Half of their suitcases must have been filled with presents; over the next days they gave little tokens to everyone connected with the Joiner Center. Most of the gifts were small straw Vietnamese masks.

That weekend we drove out to Concord, a visiting fireman's tour. It was a lush New England summer day and the countryside seemed particularly clean and green after the week in Dorchester; even the highway median had been planted in a rainbow of wildflowers. As at the airport, I felt compelled to try and see the American landscape as I imagined the Vietnamese would see it, or at least Le Minh Khue, since she and Lady Borton, a Quaker who'd lived in and written about Vietnam for twenty-five years, had come in my car. Lady had spent the war in Vietnam, doing medical work in Quang Ngai province with the American Friends Service Committee. Since then she'd gone back and forth to Vietnam many times. Her Vietnamese was fluent.

We walked over the neat lawns and under the shade of the large oaks at Concord. Huu Thinh was a poet who had risen from private to Lieutenant Colonel in the North Vietnamese Army during the war; now he was editor-in-chief of *Van Nghe*, *Arts and Letters*, Vietnam's premier literary journal. He stared at everything intently with both a soldier's and a poet's eyes, as if trying to take in both the surface terrain and its subtler connotations.

When he'd arrived he had emptied his suitcase of gifts for us—now he seemed determined to carry back every conversation, explanation and sight he experienced, to copy by hand nothing less then the whole country into the small notebook he took every place with him. I liked him very much, and his curiosity touched off a didactic urge in me so that I began acting as tour guide. After I'd described the actions of the Minutemen, or at least as much as I could remember from fourth grade and the "Midnight Ride of Paul Revere," the Vietnamese began calling them guerrillas. "Did the guerrillas hide behind these walls? Where did they keep their weapons hidden?" At the statue of the Minuteman, Khue looked up and smiled wryly and said something in Victnamese that made Lady Borton laugh. "She says he's too beautifully dressed for a guerrilla," Lady said.

She would know, I thought. I felt good about Khue's remark: it was the first time she'd said anything mildly sarcastic. Perhaps she was starting to relax. We were all suddenly feeling a new ease with each other: the drive and the walk and the gesture of making and accepting the comparison of revolutions relaxing us.

A park guide, beautifully dressed as a Minuteman, came over to us. He was a middle aged man, balding, the white hair swept thinly over his scalp revealed when he removed the tricorner hat and wiped his brow. "Where are you folks from?" he asked.

"They're visiting from Vietnam," David Hunt, co-director of the Joiner Center, explained. "They're writers, from Hanoi. Veterans from the other side of the war," he added, and we could see that what he wanted was a reaction from this man dressed as a patriot. I felt myself tense a little, hoping that whatever the reaction it wouldn't disturb the day. "Really," the Minuteman said. "I was in Vietnam." Weigl and I looked at each other; I could see him tensing also. "The A Shau," the Minuteman said. I looked nervously at the musket he was holding. But he didn't seem angry or even overly impressed, and when Thieu translated to Huu Thinh and Le Minh Khue, they beamed as if they'd met a long lost comrade-in-arms; Khue staring in surprise, with a small smile at this beautiful American guerrilla who'd come to her country. They shook hands. In the crack of that second, cheap visual symbolism and all, I felt a great surge of anger, the kind of anger I'd had when I'd come back from the war and begun protesting against it: a rage at the waste of ourselves, the waste of fighting these people who suddenly seemed parts of myself I hadn't realized were missing.

The Minuteman was well informed and he gave a detailed analysis of the battle as Huu Thinh scribbled furiously. When he was finished, he gave Thinh his card: he was chair of the history department at Boston College. In Vietnam, he'd been a Green Beret captain. So we come to Concord, I thought, and the Minuteman turns out to be a guerrilla and a Vietnam vet, and there was no part of us not touched by this. Huu Thinh tried on his tricorner hat and Thieu took his musket. They posed for pictures together and then Thieu took Weigl prisoner for the camera, making him raise his hands, pointing the musket at Weigl's back and then resting the barrel down between his cheeks, poking him as Khue laughed and then bit her lip, as if unsure if she should.

In the car, she told me about her daily schedule at home. She worked all day as an editor at the Vietnam Writers Association Publishing House, though she also did freelance articles for extra money. At home—her husband was a university professor and she had a ten-year-old daughter—she did all the cooking and house work. She didn't get to her own writing until eleven in the evening—she would work from then until three. "It's my time to be alone with the secret life of my writing, the time I don't share with anyone."

"Why is it?" I asked her, "that the most important part of ourselves, the part where our writing comes from, is a secret we can't share with the people we love, but we can put it on the page and share it with strangers?"

Her face in the rearview mirror suddenly looked indescribably sad. She said nothing, only nodded and a silence fell over us. On our way out, we stopped at a roadside gift and vegetable store and I bought some linen napkins hand embroidered with country scenes, and put them into a gift bag for Khue. It hardly seemed enough. For the rest of the trip, whenever we got out of the car, she carried that bag with her.

I caught her looking at me curiously a few days later as I sat with her and Lady Borton around the kitchen table in Kevin and Leslie's house. I asked her if she still wrote about the war. "To tell you the truth," she said, "I'm sick of it." I laughed and we talked about writing again. We had both written stories in which people found the bones of war casualties, in which characters tore the bones of the dead from the earth. We had both questioned the good of continually reaching our hands into the earth, pulling out what was rotting in memory, stories about terrible things.

She began to talk about her time in the war. The orphaned daughter of school teachers, she had left her aunt and uncle's home when she was fifteen to join the North Vietnamese Army; she and most of her high school friends had gone together. They'd been put in a young volunteers' brigade and sent to work in a sapper group, repairing the bomb craters we'd blow in the road, shifting dirt and rock and ordnance with their bare hands: they had to learn to defuse or explode the unexploded bombs. "Many of us died," she said simply. The bombing was constant and they were also showered with chemicals, napalmed, strafed.

She asked what I had done, and when I told her, hesitantly, that I'd been in a helicopter crew, she smiled at me grimly and said she was very afraid of the helicopters; they came down.

"I was scared for the same reason."

At one time, I'd flown on missions in and out of Khe Sanh and around that area, over the jungle that hid the Trail. My year intersected one of the years she'd been there and so more than likely we'd been very near each other at times during the war. When I told her that, we were silent a moment and then she rested her hand on my arm, a gesture of comfort and connection. At her touch an image came vividly into my mind as if she'd put it through my skin: I remembered how once we were flying over that triple canopied jungle when we received a fire mission—a recon patrol had spotted an enemy unit moving on the trail under the trees. I'd fired down blindly into the blank green below, my tracers disappearing into it as if absorbed. A picture of this woman sitting in front of me now, crouched under the leaves, hiding from my fire, came into my mind and I felt a pang of grief and horror that was as fresh and real as if I'd just seen the body of a loved one. I thought of how we would have looked for each other during the war, Khue on the ground, peering up in fear and hate; me in the air, staring down, my eyes aching with fatigue and hate, searching for her on the ground. How much we had wanted to see each other, I thought. We looked at each other and then the two of us smiled, our faces emerging across the space of the kitchen table as if from leaves or sky.

"Did you ever see any Americans?" I asked.

"Only some prisoners once, being taken north." And once, near Khe Sanh, she and some of her girl friends had spied on the G.I.'s taking showers. "But I was too far away to see anything," she said wistfully.

"You were ghosts to us too," I said.

Yusef Komunyakaa, the poet, had come to Concord with us; now he was leaving—he'd only been able to stay for

a few days. He'd met the Vietnamese before also, in
Hanoi, and I could see how much they liked him, a
quiet, shy man who would only let the wild-assed
hipster persona out in his poetry: in person he was given
to long lovely academic mumblings and digressions
broken by self-conscious chuckles. I'd gone with him
and the Vietnamese to a jazz performance by Stanley
Turrentine; he'd been anxious to take them, as if jazz
were his Concord and Lexington. More. He'd watched
them listening, letting Turrentine's sax tell them
whatever he wanted to say about himself but couldn't.
Now he was leaving, and on the porch Thieu and Huu
Thinh got up and danced and sang for him, a traditional
village song about a lover's departure, a gift of music
given back. It was a woman's song, and they were sly and
teasing with that, but Huu Thinh's voice was quaver-
ingly beautiful and full of love for this music, the need
to have Yusef love it also. He danced gracefully, his eyes
fixed to Yusef's, his hands waving him his heart.

Before the dancing, Yusef had told Huu Thinh about his
brother, lost, his mind still locked into the war. Huu
Thinh nodded. One of his own brothers had died in the
war, he said, and the other was still disturbed and
institutionalized. Then Carolyn talked about the way
her first husband had been ruined in the war and Larry
told Thinh how his younger brother had been wounded
body and soul and come back and disappeared into
America, as if he was an MIA, and George Evans told
him how many of his friends from childhood had died

in the war, and Khue said hers also, and I thought about a boy who died in my place on a mission I was supposed to fly and the image that always comes back to me started to form then, on the porch: the tangle of dead rooted around my feet on a helicopter deck. Then Thieu said he'd been too young but remembered how when his father came back—his village had lost seventy out of a hundred and fifty soldiers who'd gone south—he never spoke about it, but each night when he thought Thieu was asleep he'd come into his son's bed and hold him tightly. Huu Thinh stared at us. Drink, he said. I command it. Drink.

There are so many wasted lives between us, George Evans would write later, *that only beauty makes sense.*

He and Thinh touched each other deeply in many ways. Evans, who had been a medic, was a San Francisco poet in the fine old hip North Beach, Kerouac and Cassady, meaning of the word, a stocky man with a black goatee and a lived in face and a booming genuinely delighted laugh. "He's a beautiful cat," he said of Huu Thinh. Huu Thinh didn't speak English, though by the end of a week he was already developing a working vocabulary and a special language with George. The two of them would put their heads together like conspirators, Huu Thinh murmuring and nodding vigorously as Evans showed him a poem or a building or a part of the garden; you could see Huu Thinh catching it from the same angle, catching the same twist. Evans had studied Chinese calligraphy in Japan—when he had difficulty communicating a particular concept he would delicately draw a Chinese character that encapsulated something only he and Huu Thinh would see and Huu Thinh would take the pen and draw another character and they'd look at each other and laugh, linked by the swirls and lines on the paper.

At midweek, George and I, Larry Heinemann, Lady Borton and Leslie Bowen took Huu Thinh and Thieu and Khue to the Museum of Fine Arts. Huu Thinh was effusive, perhaps diplomatically, in his praise of the museum and the exhibits, comparing it favorably to the Hermitage, which he'd visited when he was in Moscow. We saw a retrospective of American watercolorists. Huu Thinh stared at each painting intently as if trying to physically absorb it; then he'd ask questions and write in his notebook with the methodical thoroughness and patience of an experienced guerrilla. Evans and Thieu took off, and Le Minh Khue wandered around with Lady Borton, though occasionally she would seek me out, take my arm and bring me silently in front of a picture she wanted me to see: mostly Hoppers or Wyeths, invariably depictions of dark isolation and loneliness. Evans and Thieu found us again—they had been to the contemporary art exhibit and insisted on taking us there. I had reservations—perhaps Thinh's taste in art was conservative. But as Evans, his deep laugh echoing happily against the high white walls, showed them a canvas depicting the dangling feet of a hanged man, a metal ball on the floor that changed shape according to the angle at which it was viewed, a pattern of merging shadows created by a mobile made from a wire chair hung from the ceiling, I saw light break on Huu Thinh's face, genuine delight at art, at unexpected possibilities.

On the way out, Khue spotted a statue of a headless nude woman with firm massive breasts and heroic hips. She tugged Thieu's sleeve and insisted on having a photo taken of herself posed next to the nude. She stood with her slight figure dwarfed and smiled a shyly triumphant smile; it was her version of Thieu's grin when he'd stepped off the plane like a conqueror or liberator: a smile of victory over the large.

It hurt badly to leave. George and Carolyn and I sat on the porch and drank with Huu Thinh and Thieu and Khue. The Vietnamese were staying on, then going to New York and Washington, but the program for the American writers was over—I would leave for Europe a day after I got back. Carolyn was sleepy and left after a time and the five of us sat, listening to the wind chimes.

We'd all come to feel sealed to each other and the thought of departure was more painful than I'd imagined it could be, as if whatever had come full cycle in us was about to be pulled asunder again. We were looking at each other's faces in the moonlight, I thought, the way I had looked at the photograph of my mother at her father's grave in Poland, as if at evidence that our own past existed. We were closer to each other than we could ever be, ever again, to our own countrymen—we shared between us another country and still moved through the world remembering the lessons we'd brought back from it: the ability to read the terrain, the deadly earth we flew over or walked on or from which we pulled unexploded bombs, the understanding of what it cost to see only what you wanted to see on or in or above that ground. When she was nineteen and still on the Trails, Khue had told me, she published her first story, an account of life in the youth brigades. She'd tried to put everything into the story, both the terror and the love; she found that the only way she could do it was by shining an intense light on a small area... She would describe the surface, reconfigure it so that your eyes could see it, so that you would understand what lay beneath it, ready to explode. It was a way of looking at the world and seeing connections and patterns that she discovered she possessed: the qualities of a good sapper.

I thought about the first story I'd published when I got back from the war, a little animal parable about G.I.'s trying to exterminate rats who wouldn't die; they'd called the rats gooks. The story had come to me from an experience that itself had come to stand in my mind for the war, and that I'd thought could stand in anyone's mind for the war, if I did it right. I'd wanted—or become conscious in the writing of the story of wanting—to depict the brutality of that small massacre graphically enough to evoke the larger massacres and moral erosion of the war, in the same way that seeing the event had connected to certain images in my mind: a line of prisoners held by Nung mercenaries who had secured them into a grotesque coffle by punching a wire through their cheeks, a woman's blood fanning into brown paddy water, the secondary memories of the slaughter at My Lai: those photographs in *Life* whose context my own memories could supply—and behind that, images of Nazis shooting people into ditches. Now, recently, I'd published a story about a woman who finds the bones of a murdered Civil War prisoner on a Maryland beach: the things that wouldn't go away rising to the surface of the earth, and in the collection Khue published that year she'd included a story about two viciously amoral Hanoi con men, father and son, who find and try to sell the bones of an American G.I. Soon the ghost of a black soldier, skeletal and ghastly and stinking of rot, begins to haunt their dreams, dances around their beds at night, crouches in the rafters, laughing maniacally at them until they light incense to him, send him home, put him to rest...we didn't so much want as needed to open bags of bones that would flesh into many faces, into the particular face that would seep into people's dreams like a ghost they would follow into their own hearts and something fundamental in them would shift and change. That's all.

That need, more than the war itself, our fixed juxtaposition under and above the jungle canopy; that inability to forget the cost of lies and wishful thinking, that need to make you *see*, linked us like twins separated by the bulge of the earth, weepers at the edge of the parade, though—as much as I wanted symmetry—I knew what it cost me and what it cost Le Minh Khue to get to that point was as disproportionate as a comparison of the casualties of the war—the 58,000 Americans to the four million Vietnamese—or of my months at war to her years. Under the bombing, she'd told me, the girls would huddle together in their bunkers and caves, like the children my mother told me about who huddled in a cellar in Kolno, their ears and mouths bleeding from the shock. Then they would emerge and defuse or blow up the unexploded bombs. She'd done that for years. She was still doing that. Still smoothing the earth into peace. And still wounding it again. Still digging into the ground and unearthing bones so they could be seen in the light, and prayed to, and brought to rest in the world she'd seen her generation die in the jungle to make, because that's what she has to do, because she is a serious person, because that's what we've been left alive to do.

"I spent twenty-six years in the jungle," Huu Thinh said, handing me a beer. "I was thirty years old before I ever kissed a woman." To forget war was good, he nodded, putting one hand on my arm and one on George's. But not to forget what had been paid.

Once, during a bombing, he said, his comrades had covered his body with their own so he could finish writing a poem he'd started. Who was left now who can understand the language in which such a poem is written?

"Pass the Scotch," George Evans said. He filled our glasses and we toasted each other silently and drank and drank more and he and I made drunken, silly speeches, trying to express what he would only get right later, in a poem he'd write about taking the Vietnamese to a Japanese rock garden, in words that on the last night were still held unformed in the air, in the steady tolling of the wind chimes:

We entered the garden by chance. We were like the rocks there, plucked from some other place to be translated by circumstance into another tongue. And in the silent crashing of stone waterfalls, and rising of inanimate objects into music, we remembered there was a time we would have killed each other.

We went into the house and brought out more scotch and bourbon. Thieu brought some cucumbers and a tall clear bottle of *nuoc mam*, fish sauce, that he put on the wicker table next to Huu Thinh. Its strong sharp smell wafted to me: it was a smell that would always conjure Vietnam to me, that, along with several words and sounds and colors, had become the physical traces of memory. After a while Huu Thinh sliced the cucumber, put the slices on a small white plate and offered it first to me, on his left, and then to George, to my right, and then to Thieu and Khue. Then he gestured at me to give him my glass. I did and he picked up the bottle of *nuoc mam* and poured, filling half my glass. He handed it back, the rancid anchovy smell making my nostrils sting. I thought, OK, it was a ceremony, the drinking of the fish sauce: I'd take the country into me and I raised the glass and gulped it down. It tasted like it smelled. I gave the glass back to him. Huu Thinh filled it and passed it to George, who looked at me. "I think it's the custom," I said, and he shrugged and drank it and handed the glass to Thieu. Huu Thinh leaned over and filled it again. Thieu tilted his glass and drank deeply and then spewed it out.

"That's fucking fish sauce," he said.

We looked at each other, the liquid rot taste of the past still in our mouths, and we burst into laughter, expressions of delighted recognition opening on our faces: we'd finally made a new legend for each other.

RUMORS: STONE

My grandmother Sarah Gittel gave birth to thirteen
children, but six died during or immediately after birth
or from illness. Except for her son Dov, she treated the
survivors with a suspicious irritation. Whenever she
looked at them, a cold, transparent carapace formed
over her eyes, like something sliding up from her heart.
After the stillborn birth of her third child, she'd seized
the small corpse from Slava, the Polish midwife, and
began kissing and panting over the child's icy flesh,
rubbing its limbs between her hands. Slava had to tear
the corpse away from her hands as she'd torn it from the
grip of her body. When her fourth child was also
stillborn, she tried to bite into her own wrists, smiling
up at Slava, holding her own white arm like a bone.
Cold, she said, and bared her teeth. Slava saw Sarah
Gittel's soul turn into a fluttering bird trying to escape
from her eyes. Instructing her sister Yasha to hold her
down, she went outside and found a stone, heated it on
the stove, wrapped it in swaddling and brought it to
Sarah Gittel. She allowed Sarah Gittel to hold the solid
form and feel the heat through the cloth, then snatched

it quickly away. You see, she said, your baby is alive. At that instant Slava saw an image of her own hands molding lumps of bloody flesh to life and the notion came to her that she could stroke the stone to existence, knead its heat to flesh, a thought of such terrible arrogance she knew it must have been put into her mind by the dybbuk that had entered Sarah Gittel at the moment of her body's openness; she'd seen it happen before to her Jewish patients. Sarah Gittel grabbed the heated stone back from Slava with a superhuman strength. She opened the cloth, laughed wildly and pressed her lips to the surface of the rock, burning them. Then she lay back against the pillows, pushing the stone to her breast, murmuring in a strange drone through the ring of new blisters on her lips.

The first child not stillborn was a girl, Bechele, who later died in the great influenza epidemic. The first time Sarah Gittel nursed the infant, she felt its lips turn into a hot ring of stone at her nipple and shrieked. After that, her children were given over to Slava's sister Yasha, a wet nurse.

My mother spent the first five years of her life in the cramped dark house of the two sisters. She would suck at one of Yasha's breasts while Yasha's daughter Wanda hung at the other, black hair and blond hair. At night, by the fire, Yasha would tell both girls stories from the Bible, as well as stories of the witches and demons who inhabited the forests around Kolno. On each Jewish Sabbath, Yasha would tell my mother the story of Eve, the first woman, exiled from paradise for what Yasha described as the sin of wanting to name names. Then my mother would be washed and scrubbed with cold well water, dressed in the clothing Yasha only took out for that day, taken to her real house and presented to her mother, as if a decision were to be made. Sarah Gittel would look at her coldly, as if she was just another stone brought to fool her.

THE KOLNO BOOK

My mother's stories, like the best fiction, never tied
everything together too neatly and usually left several
unanswered questions in the listener's mind. What
happened then, I always asked? The year before she'd
died, I'd tape-recorded some of her stories. When I
brought the machine into her room she looked at me
and nodded, as if to say: so you finally understand what
will happen to me. With the machine giving me the
illusion of professional control and detachment, I tried
to organize and structure her responses and lead them
to an ending that would neatly tie up all the loose ends.
But her answers, the stories, would merge together,
connect and finally disconnect as randomly as the flow
of memory. What was your house made of in Kolno? I
asked. Wood or I think stone. The doors were big, huge.
What did your father do? I was his favorite. I'd lie on his
chest and play with his beard. My mother would tell me
not to, she was jealous, but I was his pet.

My father's family, the Karlinskys, was also from
some place in Russia, she said vaguely. The Jews in

Kolno lived in an uneasy peace with their Polish neighbors, a completely segregated, self-sufficient existence: they spoke Yiddish among themselves, Polish, Russian and German only to the gentiles. The name Brickman, her maiden name, came from Van Bryckman, a Dutch name, which meant the family had emigrated to Poland from Holland, and, according to her brother Herman, was originally a Sephardic family, since the Dutch Jews had come up from Spain after the Expulsion. Her mother was a cold, aloof woman who refused to nurse her own children: she'd sent my mother away to a wet nurse the first four years of her life. She was also perhaps a little crazy, my mother thought, from losing so many children. Her mother's family name was Rosenfeld; there were cousins in Kolno also from the maternal side, the Lubels. The village had been caught up in the fighting between the Germans and Poles and Russians. Or there had been a pogrom. Or perhaps both: she remembered hiding in the cellar with her family and listening to shooting and screams in the streets: at one point she and her younger brother had peeked out and seen people being shot, men running, blood flowing in the gutter. They'd stayed so long without water, they had to drink their own urine. She remembered she'd gotten her first menstruation while in hiding. Finally there were only her mother, father and younger brother left. The other children had either left for America or died. Her older brothers, she thought, may have been involved in some sort of revolutionary politics. Is that why they had to flee? Maybe—why not, if that's what I wanted to hear. But she remembers vividly how her next older sister died of the flu: a beautiful young woman, she'd taken the illness from my mother and died in her place. And after her father died, she and her mother and younger brother finally left to join her other brothers and sisters in America.

Why didn't your father go? I'd asked her. Because of his stroke. How did he get a stroke? A stroke is a stroke. One day during or before the fighting my brother hurt his hand very seriously so it was rotting, and my father dragged him by sled through snow and forest to a doctor. It was a terrible journey and when he came back he had a stroke and his arm became stiff. His right arm, I think—what's the difference? We heard someone attacked him. What could we do? After he died we were poor, and the boys in America sent for us. We had to buy potatoes from the peasants and sell them in the market square to live. Why do you want to know what happened to him in the forest? What happened, happened. Did he know the way because he was a smuggler? Who knows? What are you doing, is that machine working or is all this for nothing?

It's working, I'd said.

On the day he died, her father called her into his room and his paralyzed arm came to life as if he were trying to point a direction for her. She and her mother and younger brother were the last ones to leave Kolno for America: on the ship, her mother, an orthodox woman, threw her wig into the ocean, a gesture of liberation that always stayed in my mother's mind: a few years later, still a teenager, she left home herself, refusing to work for her brothers; instead she got her own apartment and job. Her boss, a young ex-boxer who was in the process of divorcing his first wife, became my father.

That's the ending, she told me. Stories have to end, what more do you want? How should she know if any were left behind, caught in the Holocaust? Probably everybody got out; she didn't know what had happened to anyone else. Why bring it up? Europe was covered with blood. Her other cousins, most of whom lived in the bigger town of Lomza, were Zionists: they all went to Palestine in the twenties—I'd met them in Israel, hadn't I? But what about Albert Rosenfeld? I asked. Albert lived in France now: I'd met him briefly when I was eighteen and could remember vaguely a story about him escaping from a boxcar on the way to a death camp. Yes, she said, Albert had been there in the war; she thought he'd gone to Treblinka, she wasn't sure. But she thought he was the only one. And Kolno? Who knew? She didn't like to think about it.

Once, when I was living in Jerusalem, she came to Israel on a two week tour and we went to Yad Vashem, the Holocaust memorial, where I understood a record was kept of all the Jewish towns and villages destroyed during the war. I asked a curator, an old man who wore a skullcap and a gray smock, if there was any record of Kolno, and my mother told him where the town was located. Of course, there must be, he said. He came back in minutes with a black bound book. Here, he said, and held it out to my mother. She hesitated for a few seconds, then grasped the book firmly with both hands, as if she were pulling something out of time.

I knew then that a book about Kolno existed: I'd seen it but couldn't remember much about it. At the time I'd skimmed through it, saw photos of Zionist groups and people in high collars and dark clothes posing stiffly, like pictures of families in the Old West. I did know that someone in our family had a copy of that book, and finally tracked it down to a cousin in New York. Gail, who is of my generation, said she'd be glad to send it, or a photocopy, to me, and then we talked a little about my plans to go to Kolno. She wished she could go. We talked a little about her uncle Bernie, who had given her the book. Bernie had been born in Kolno. He'd gone back to Poland last year, but had not gone to the town: it was out of the way and hard to get to. That probably wasn't the only reason, I suggested: my mother had always refused to go there. Gail agreed. Her grandfather, my mother's brother David, now dead also, had told her not to go to Poland when she was in Europe. He hated the Poles, she said. He had no good memories of the place. My mother, I said to her, always told me that Europe dripped with blood.

I'd found the town on a map with some difficulty— it was not on the map in the guidebook to Poland I'd bought, or any of the others I'd seen in the bookstore, and for a second I'd considered the idea that it didn't exist: another long-accepted myth called into doubt. It wasn't until I'd gotten a Michelin road map that I was able to find the town, the name solidly there, under a black dot. The map, and the guidebook, and the Polish history I'd started to read in fact confirmed other elements of her stories. Kolno was in northeastern Poland, on the southern edge of the Piska forest, not far from the border with the new country of Belarus, southeast of Gdansk, west of Bialystok. At the time my mother lived there it would, in fact, have been near the Danzig corridor and East Prussia, that part of Germany digitated into Poland. Whatever fictions my mother had created were at least fastened to a real landscape it was possible to see and touch.

Finally, the Kolno book came from Gail. On the front page were listed the names of the 24 members of its editorial board, the Israeli and American survivors who had compiled the book. Among them were Kelman Karlinsky, Pinchas Lubel, Arieh Rosenfeld.

The book had arrived a week before I left for Boston, on the trip where I'd meet the Vietnamese writers. At home I settled down to glance through it, though soon I was drawn into it, as if into a pit. The history of the Jewish community of Kolno began bleakly and ended horribly. Yad Vashem, as I understood it, wanted to have a book for each Jewish community that had been wiped out, and the preservation of Kolno on paper was an impressively thorough act of witness. Each chapter was an account by an individual who had put into writing his or her memories of the town and its Jewish population at different times and in different aspects: its physical geography, schools and religious and charitable institutions, the ways people made their livings. The details were remembered with a kind of loving thoroughness that had the effect of creating a sense of foreboding in me as I read on: only destroyed things were remembered in such detail. I felt as if I was hearing an elaborate story about a family vacation, with its pleasures and small mishaps, that I knew was going to end so terribly that those aspects would become moot. That sense of curse hung over even the most innocuous or even rapturous recollections of everyday life in the book: a sense of curse and sometimes a literal curse, as when Herschel Kolinsky, who after writing of the bucolic setting and rural pleasures of the town ended his article with a list of those he wanted remembered:

My sister, Shayne, her husband Matys Kalman, and five children, killed in the town of Szcuczyn by the Germans and Poles;

My sister, Neshke Chmiel, with two children, killed in Kolno;

My brother, Moshe Chaim Kolinsky, wife Blume and two children, killed in Szcuczyn;

My baby sister Cyvia, her husband Yankel Crystal, with two children, killed in Kolno.

I will never forgive your murderers! I will never forget you!

RUMORS: THE SMUGGLER'S DAUGHTER

The light—the flickering flame of a candle, the leaps and fades of memory—plays on the screen. Light and shadow. In the cart next to her father's slim perched form, his secrets lying cool on her body, my mother lies back and closes her eyes and feels the vibrations pass into her body. The wheels hit a rut, the cart leaps from the earth. She opens her eyes and claps her hands over her ears and lets blue sky and rolling white clouds fill her vision; it is as if she is tumbling through the sky.

What do borders mean to birds? she remembers her brother Dov saying to her once: *our father's a creature of the air, little one.* In her mind she sees a tiny black winged form looping on a sky white as parchment, her father's bony face and thin hawk's nose and deep shadowed black eyes peering down at fields and forests. At home, in the evenings when he would lie down, she'd push under his arm the way she'd seen ducklings press against their mother's wings. The soft feathers of his beard would tickle her cheeks. She'd hear his heartbeat muffled under the thick down of his velvet robe.

At the check point she smiles sweetly at soldiers and custom agents and lets them pinch her cheeks. The cart is empty; when her father is asked what he brought over, he says, dried mushrooms, and gives the guards the papers he carries. After they pass, he places his hand lightly on her head and looks at her with a strange sadness. She glows under his touch, but the look and the uniforms suddenly scare her, remind her of the stories Dov had told her about the mounted policeman, Tobie, and his jail at the edge of Kolno, at the edge of the Piska forest. He would bring the smugglers he bagged and clip their wings there, Dov said. She saw broken bodies pinned to dark wet walls.

What do borders mean to birds? Borders trench her country, her town, her house, her heart, deep aching ruts: how can she lift above what's been scored inside? On each side of the line she's a different person, a story flowing to the shape of a body, like cloth. *Let Zak go shit in the ocean,* her mother said. *How will you bring the sample over?*

Magic, her father had said.

They ride into Bialystok, her father tall and calm in his great black coat, his square linen cap, the hawk-tension of his posture. Suddenly they're surrounded by flocks of black-clad Jews, screeching like crows, wheeling, their faces stamped with the panic of birds who have lost the secret of flight. The air smells dry and rotten as if brushed by a desert wind and the faint whiff of carrion. She clings to her father's arm. Young men, shaven Jews, their faces hard and mocking, stand on the corners, yell rhyming Yiddish phrases to her in a city slang she doesn't understand. Young women, their faces painted, wink at her from dark windows. Her father pulls the reins, and they stop and dismount. A fat man in a leather apron nods and takes the rein, touches the brim of his hat in salute. They walk across the street towards a crumbling brick building. In front of it more young men and women perch at sidewalk tables, glasses of tea steaming in front of them, their faces narrow and strained. A troop of street actors, *Kassa*, suddenly whirls through the street. The people on the sidewalks laugh and applaud. Down with the blackleg scabs, a boy in a skull mask, a skeleton's rib-bones painted on his vest, screams. She feels drawn towards the actors, their intent expressions, the outrageous freedom of their costumes. A desire to join them, as sudden and wild as their mad whirl through the street, slips into her heart. It frightens her more than anything she has seen. Her father stands watching for a moment, a slight, knowing smile on his lips that her mind clings to like the safety of a secret place. Her hand clutches his arm.

Magic. She thinks of the hot room in Danzig; how the woman winding the linen around her body had winked at her. Tight and smooth as a lover's embrace, girl; that's the way. She'd felt the warm cloth weave into her own skin, felt dizzy with happiness at her father's trust, his wrapping of her to himself. His magic.

The performers drift away. Snippets of conversation float to her ears from the young people at the sidewalk tables. She hears words she's heard in her brother's mouth hatch from their mouths. Agitation, says a girl with glowing green eyes, tossing her tangled red hair. Action, a tall boy, Dov's age, says and winks at her. *Kassa*, he whispers. Suddenly, as if he were a curse called up by the boy's wink or words, a man dressed as a spider leaps in front of her and begins to cavort crazily, his face crusted with white paint, black fangs dripping with venom painted under his lips. Four lifeless but madly bobbing legs are fastened to each side of the spider's shirt. She holds her father tighter. The spider winks at her like the boy at the table, turns and begins dancing after three thin young men dressed in gray webby rags. A young boy laughs and yanks off one of the spider's legs as it goes by him. People applaud and laugh. The spider rips off another leg and begins beating the rag-draped figures with it, chasing them in a circle. White signs suddenly wink through the gathering crowd, more of Dov's words alighting on them. *Awake, Betrayal, Solidarity, Revolution.* The spider hits his victims with his torn-off leg, drives them into a dark alley. In a few seconds he comes scurrying back out, face twisted comically, his victims chasing him with his own legs. Bloodsucker, exploiter, they yell. *Kassa*, the boy at the table whispers to her again. The real under the mask of the real, he whispers. She laughs, filled again with a strange restlessness. He takes her laugh into a series of mocking caws.

Her father's face creases with sadness and disgust. She crinkles her own face in imitation. He turns, gesturing her to follow, disappears into the darkness of a cave-like entrance inside a small alley as if he's dived off the earth. Panic scurries in my mother's chest and throat like a thin dusty spider. She plunges after him. *What's a border but a choice?* her brother once said.

The walls inside the dark and narrow space are made of the same stained brick as the walls outside, but they are furred and crusted with a wet-streaked mold, the walls softening and blackening around her as she descends so the light not only darkens but seems to thicken. Particles of mossy dust float in the air, clog her throat and nostrils, make her cough and sneeze. The floor levels. They're in a cave-like room. As her eyes focus, she sees dozens of pale human forms lining the walls, writhing in the shadows, their hands fluttering over the cords that fasten their bodies to what seems to her to be great squares of web. A thump vibrates and throbs between the close walls like a heartbeat. She covers her ears, but the noise comes through her hands so the skin of her palms trembles against her ears. The figures become skinny old men with stiffly tangled beards, their faces thickened with gray dust; they become small, drained boys the age of her younger brother Yitzhak. She sees

Jews who can't fly hunched over sewing machines or webbed into the strings of looms, husked and sucked dry.

A round face smiles at them from the darkness on the other side of the cave. She sees the Kassa spider from upstairs flowing into his real form, the real under the mask of the real, pale and bloated, gliding towards her past the gray husks of his victims. His hairy white fingers swarm in the air, pinch her father's slim hand.

Zak.

Nu schoine, Ruhele, come.

Her father beckons her, his face bony and merciless. Come closer, why do you wait? He unbuttons her blouse. She struggles in his grip. He looks at her in surprise. What's this? Stand still now, *leben*, heart. Her heart is a stone in her chest. Her father reaches into her blouse and pulls out the tip of the linen wound around her middle and begins yanking her out, unraveling her; he is pulling her fluttering soul. She feels it loosen and move out from under her heart, pure and gleaming in the dusty gloom. Zak touches it and sniffs it and licks it with his moist pink tongue. He looks at her strangely.

Your daughter is getting too old for this function.

She's a baby.

The spider caresses the cloth. She feels his fingers, as if on her skin. Father draws her back, buttoning her blouse thoughtfully. He smiles at her and pats her hair.

Wait outside for me, *leben*.

As she walks, she looks back into the dark in the rear of the room and sees her father and the spider, their figures bending and wavering in the shadows, their faces fluid. Smiles wiggle into frowns, frowns dissolve into laughter. In the dim light under the earth, she sees her father change and change and change.

Agitation, she whispers.

She begins to run, spiraling up to the light of the sky, bursting into the glowing day. The light outside polishes the surface of objects and hurts her eyes. She can't stop the race of her thoughts. Her mind teems with thoughts that scream and shove for attention like the crowds around her. Betrayal, she whispers. Awaken. The city vibrates around her as if shaking itself free of invisible strands.

UNWELCOME GUESTS

The first part of the memorial book was made of reminiscences, by people who had lived there, of life in Kolno before the second World War. They described a small town of cobblestone and dirt streets and intricate relationships that existed in a landscape of great natural beauty, among fields and forests and streams, and in a tradition of intolerance and separation. Jews had lived in Kolno for about two hundred years, "at first as unwelcome guests and later as untolerated citizens," a statement which could very well describe the whole pattern of Jewish life in Poland, from the time the first Jews were invited by the monarchy to come fill the gap, economic and social, between the aristocracy and the peasantry, to provide goods, services and capital, to be hated and resented by one group, despised by the other, regarded as alien by both.

At the time my mother would have lived there, Kolno, situated as it was near East Prussia and the Danzig Corridor, was one of those points where illegal "travel agents" arranged border crossings of people trying to get out of Russia (Poland was under Russian rule until after the First World War) and emigrate, mostly to the United States. The town, like many other towns and cities in the Pale, was mostly Jewish—three thousand of its five thousand inhabitants. They lived in a strict legal, cultural, religious, economic and linguistic apartheid which undoubtedly added to the view the Poles and Russians had of the Jews—and the Jews had of themselves—as outsiders. "There was very little contact between the Jewish and Polish populations in Kolno," wrote Eric Sosnow. "The Jews organized their lives, successfully, on a full self-sufficient basis. Jewish children were educated at the Jewish religious school or at the government school for Jewish children. For a short time Kolno had a Polish secondary school...[it] was closed in 1927, when the proportion of Jewish children had reached one-third of all the pupils. This caused the local government to withdraw its support...as far as I remember, this short episode...brought Jewish and Polish children together for the first and only time."

Most Jewish boys—the girls were rarely allowed to attend school—received their educations in religious schools, in the *Cheder*, and several of the accounts mention a remarkable teacher, a crippled, hunchbacked dwarf, about three feet tall, named Gedalie Ali. He was a self-taught scholar who started the first secular *Cheder* and who was loved by generations of students: "he sought to inculcate his pupils with a...desire to strive for knowledge and to forsake superstition," wrote Herschel Kolinsky.

Education even for boys was further restricted by quotas on the number of Jews allowed in university and in secondary schools: to get into these you needed to be not only smarter than the Christian students, but also fairly well-off, both because of living expenses and because of the necessary bribes. The majority of Jews in Kolno, as in the rest of the Pale, were poor; the majority, therefore, were uneducated. Sosnow, who came from a wealthier family than many and who was able to get into the university quota for Jews, tells of helping the Bund, the Jewish Socialist organization whose ideology called for Jewish autonomy in Poland, organize classes for working-class Jews in Kolno; "the people who came to the classes spoke Yiddish, their mother tongue...and used Polish as a necessary auxiliary language...in this way we were able to conduct our educational work without interference from the Poles, who kept a watchful eye on any organization doing work which could be interpreted as political."

The Jews of Kolno governed themselves through the *Kehilah*, the Central Office of the Jewish Community, which took responsibility for hiring rabbis and constructing synagogues, for schools, for judging civil cases among the Jews, and which offered a forum for the hotbed of Jewish political and religious movements that flourished in Poland and in Kolno: the Socialist Bund, the Zionists, the communists, the various religious movements—hasidim, mitnagdim, cabbalists and more. They represented the ideological or intellectual or spiritual choices of Jewish life—although the choice for many was simply to survive or the hope, nearly a religious belief itself, of one day getting to America. Although the memorial book doesn't detail conditions elsewhere in the Pale, what prevailed in Kolno when my mother was growing up was a microcosm of Jewish life in much of the Jewish reserve of the Russian empire.

It was a good place to leave. The non-Jewish socialists and communists didn't regard the Jewish workers as real revolutionary material because there were very few factory workers among them (except in Bialystok); yet the activist Karl Kautsky noted that "if the Russian proletariat is more exploited than any other proletariat, there exists yet another class of workers who are still more oppressed, exploited, and ill-treated than all the others; this pariah among pariahs is the Jewish proletariat." Unable to own land, squeezed out of their role as middlemen, poverty-stricken, most Jews subsisted as "artisans"—workers in clothing and crafts, carpenters, glaziers, locksmiths, bakers, tailors, bristle workers, plasterers, cigarette workers, "raft" workers, and tanners. Often they were unemployed or subsisted on starvation wages. They worked in the cities for small jobbers, "loynketniks," who were usually other Jews since the mechanized factories that started to dominate the economy of the Pale, even when owned by Jews, commonly refused to hire Jewish workers. "The Jews are good workers," a Jewish factory owner in Smorgon complained, "but they are capable of organizing revolts against the employer, the regime, and the Czar himself." (The man who said this owned a tanning factory.

In that same town in Vilna province, according to Mendelsohn's *Class Struggle in the Pale*, there were twenty-two tanneries and 600 tanners, 400 of whom were Jews; most tanners, because of the chemicals used in the work, became invalids after ten or fifteen years. The smell that marked them became known in Poland as "Jewish funk.") Working conditions in the *loynketnik* shops were intolerable, with men, women and children laboring sixteen to eighteen hour days at clumsy wooden looms in dark, tight, unventilated warrens, or in the cigarette factories, where skeletal young girls suffered from various lung diseases brought about "by the constant inhalation of nicotine."

In these circumstances, both a large underworld—gangsters, pimps, prostitutes and smugglers—and revolutionary movements thrived. The revolutionary and strike movements were sometimes violent. Hooligans from the Jewish underworld were hired by the *loynketniks* to beat up organizers and strikers; Jewish revolutionary groups formed "*shrek-otriaden*"—"fright-detachments" or groups known as "*boeviks*"—fighters—to attack various people and targets. Hirsh Lekert, a young shoemaker, became a hero to the Jewish Bund when he attempted to assassinate the governor of Vilna. He represented the violent edge of the Jewish workers' movement, though the urge to stroke back physically was always a sub theme in Jewish ghetto politics, one that would culminate in the ghetto revolts against the Nazis and that stretched back in the yearning sensed in the legend of the golem, the perfect terrorist, a creature

sculpted out of frustration and impotence, a counter to
the image of Jew as helpless victim—the kind of
creature into which I'd once tried to shape myself. I
wondered if any of my relatives had taken part in such
activities. Why did your brothers and sisters leave
Kolno? I'd asked my mother more than once. Was it just
to get to America? Were they involved in anything
political? I don't remember, she had always answered,
her eyes shifting, as if I were an interrogator.

Making a living for the Jews in Kolno centered for
the most part around the town's market square.
Peasants would come into town to sell produce and buy
from the shops and stalls around it: the Jews of Kolno,
said Sosnow: "as many others in many Polish towns and
villages derived their living by catering to the farmers'
needs, supplying them with consumer goods and the
services of Jewish tailors, cobblers, blacksmiths,
glaziers...and so on." Part of the "so on" were horse
traders: a group of Kolno Jews became experts in the
field and sold Polish horses all over Europe. "The horse
trade was the main source of employment in Kolno,"
wrote Sosnow. "It provided a living for numerous
people—riders, stable boys, grooms, etc." The riders
would collect the horses from distant markets and ride
them, bare-back, to Kolno where the stable boys
prepared them for export. The best riders would qualify
for traveling abroad and accompany the horses, by rail
or sea, to their final destination.

My mother had remembered the prevalence of
smuggling correctly also. There was a great deal of cross-

border trading and smuggling: East Prussia was seven kilometers away. The occupation was apparently common but not winked at by the authorities: she had told me she remembered seeing her father arrested and jailed for smuggling. "In the center...facing the highway leading to Lomza...were the barracks of the Mounted Border Police, called the *Objesczyki*," writes Kolinsky..."those barracks used to be the Headquarters of the Gendarmerie, the forerunners of the Gestapo, where a sergeant by the name of Tobie was in charge. He used to torture the prisoners who were sentenced for smuggling...in the night one could hear the screams of the tortured."

Smuggling, as in many border towns, was a necessity for survival, and the Pale itself was in essence a large border town, a geographic metaphor for Jewish existence: in the middle, in between nations, in between classes, *nichstihein, nichstihier*, neither here nor there, my mother would say: Jews were hated by the peasants, despised by the upper classes, pushed between forces that rubbed and polished some into saints and prophets, squeezed and misshaped others into clannish hustlers, distorted souls, golems, into the very forms the gentiles accused them of inhabiting. To survive, body and soul, people had to find a purpose, a name—religion or revolution or nationalism, though looking around at the rest of Europe, all they would see were names who in the name of their names were flinging themselves on each other like foaming, demented beasts. Looking around at the rest of Europe, the choice, for many, was to slip away to a country where they could rename and reinvent themselves, to smuggle themselves out, to cut themselves off from the past as with the stroke of an ax. To, in a word, fly.

"There was never enough work and the struggle for existence was hard," Sosnow wrote. "...On reaching the age of marriage, the established thing was to establish a small workshop or to emigrate." The Jewish community of Kolno in fact was largely subsidized by relatives who'd emigrated to America and sent money back. There were other charities as well, organized and coordinated by the *Kehilah*: about half the community was on the equivalent of welfare, which, as in the rest of the Russian-Polish Pale, meant being kept alive by donations from the rest of the community. Kolinsky describes how on each Friday professional beggars would visit each house, followed, in strict order, by women who were collecting food to give anonymously to the poorest families, followed finally by the representatives of the official social charities such as "the society for free schooling for poor children, free loans for the needy; visits to the sick; helping needy brides to marry; praying...for the very ill..."

For the most part then: a town of passionate, charitable, skeptical, humorous, bitter, tragic make-doers, of getters-by, of, in a word, relatives. The threads of my mother's stories, her rumors, settled and twined into the threads of the book; the voices in it murmured into her voice; the pictures in the book merged into her photos. Many of her stories made sense—though not some of her omissions. On page 23, in the middle of Kolinsky's account, I suddenly read this:

Let me pay tribute to an unusual family, a credit to the entire community and to Kolno in particular: the Karlinski family. The mother, widowed as a young woman, making great sacrifices, raised remarkable children. The two daughters: Sarah, an attractive brunette and Reizel, a beautiful blond, were my teachers at public school....The eldest son became the famous Jewish writer, translator and critic on the staff of the Jewish Daily "Moment" in Warsaw, writing under the pen name of "Karlinus."

Had this been my father's family? It was the right name—I knew he'd changed it from Karlinsky. And his mother's name was Sarah. It was possible, maybe even probable—the fact that both my parents came from Kolno could have been their initial commonality, the first thing that had drawn them to each other. But why wouldn't she tell me that? The answer is gone, erased with the cemetery which held my grandfather's grave, with the dwarf teacher Gedalic Ali and the children who braved being beaten by the Poles to swim in the pond called Chuszhnack, and the people who gathered mushrooms deep in the forest and took them by wagon to East Prussia and the fish importers who chopped up river ice and kept the fish embedded in them, the blocks covered with straw in their basements all summer, and the cobblers and tailors and horse traders and smugglers and revolutionaries of Kolno and the market square. Gone with Moishe Lubel who helped organize the Hand-Workers union and the Brickman who ran the bus company to Lomza, and the Yankel Brickman who my cousin Lita said her grandfather Herman told her he *felt* being rubbed from his heart when the Second World War started, and the dozens of other relatives who must have been there in those final days, in spite of my mother's hopeful, helpless revisionism.

The last chapters of the memorial book were accounts by people who had witnessed what had happened in Kolno during the Holocaust and by people from the town who returned to it after the war, in the sixties and seventies, and what had happened was as brutish and final as I'd feared it would be. By the time I put the book down, many of my questions had already been answered, and I began to reconsider my trip. I no longer knew if I wanted to go there, to be among those people. I'd thought I was numbed to Holocaust stories. But reading about Kolno filled me with an ache of grief, raw as a new wound.

"I am one of those who were not there during the 'Black Days' when those nearest and dearest to us were hurled into a common grave dug by their own hands," wrote Herschel Kolinsky. "I did not hear their prayers at the brink of the grave, but only years later—from afar— did I hear their echoes. We, who were not there, still cannot believe that the things we heard about had really taken place."

RUMORS: GOLEM

He had injured his hand, my mother said. She was vague about the details, but not about the ultimate effects of that winter wounding. And in America, years later, when he became a movie projectionist, my uncle would fall into a kind of reverie during his work, stare as if in a trance not at the screen but at the beam of light from his booth, as if it were probing and softening crusts of memory, illuminating framed scenes...

...Light flickers in through the chinks between the weathered planks. A beam falls on the open page of the prayer book and makes the letters swell and shift. Yitzhak watches glowing motes of dust swirl in the beam like something released from the book. His breath tumbles them. He looks back at Gedalie Ali, gesturing energetically at the front of the cheder. As he watches, a beam of sunlight falls on the dwarf also, burning along the edge of his hump so that for an instant Gedalie Ali, in his black gabardine, looks like a cavorting letter, a tiny, twisted Hebrew "gimmel." There had been a rhyme when he'd first learned the alphabet from this same small man. *Gimmel. Gamel. The hump of the camel.* The light engraves the teacher's lumpy, impish face into the configuration of another, unknown, letter—the dark feathery overline of the brows, the flared black half-ovals of nostrils, the deep smile grooves around the mouth. The single beam of light thickens the darkness in the rest of the long narrow room; the air is heavy with the dank wet-feather odor of twenty boys sweating in their thick black clothing. They sit transfixed by Gedalie Ali's antics. Squinting, Yitzhak sees the dwarf somehow merging with his own shadow so he grows and becomes hulking, menacing: Esau, the rude and hairy hunter; now, changing—Jacob, besting his violent brother, quick and clever.

Gedalie Ali stops and claps his large gnarled hands, then lets them dangle like oversized gloves from his small, muscular wrists. Yitzhak, at ten, is already taller than his teacher. He loves the dwarf's miniature adultness. When he was five, the Polish woman who had been his wet nurse had given him a tiny carved figure, a crouched evilly-grinning skullish-faced forest imp of great and comical ugliness that he'd loved dearly and carried secretly in his breast pocket until his mother found it and threw it away. The next year, when he had first come to the cheder, he'd thought Gedalie Ali had been fashioned especially for him.

The teacher smiles at him, tugs at a hairy lobe. Recite the passage, *leben*, heart, he says. Slake my ears.

The boys giggle. A shiver of love runs through Yitzhak, its quaver passing into the timbre of his voice.

Listen to a Jew, Gedalie Ali admonishes the class. He's panting slightly from his exertions. He puffs up his cheeks and blows out a whoosh of breath, wipes the sweat from his forehead, and turns around to open the window.

Listen to a Jew, Herschel Wolf, the baker's son who sits behind Yitzhak, whispers mockingly in Yitzhak's ear and breaks wind against the wooden bench. Giggles ripple through the room.

Rebbitzin, he whispers, poking Yitzhak in the back, hard. Tiny rabbi's little wifey, he whispers.

Gedalie Ali turns back around slowly and squints into the darkness. Which boil takes it upon itself to burst before I squeeze? he asks sadly. His eyes probe the room, fall on Herschel.

You, baker's get. Dough from the land of dough—rise.

Herschel rises, the pale flesh of his cheeks trembling.

Recite, Gedalie Ali says. Emit something now.

Herschel recites the selection awkwardly, stuttering and mispronouncing the Hebrew words. The sound of my defeat, Gedalie Ali says, wincing comically, contorting his face so that the boys, even Herschel, laugh. He winks at them, pinches the bridge of his nose and blows delicately. Never mind, child, sit, wait, music will come, even to your life—though you won't hear it if you fart against wood. Now recite, all of you, he says, quickly, sing and drown the misshapen dwarves and halflings this one tries to bring into the world—drown them with the torrent of your words, drown them before they struggle to a monstrous life, I tell you. As the boys laugh and chant raucously, Gedalie Ali listens, one hand behind his ear, his face comically contorted as if in pain.

Reuben Pearle, his eyes worried, appears in the door and gestures to Gedalie Ali. Yitzhak watches the tall horse dealer and the small teacher murmur together, framed by the doorway, the other boys nudging each other at the sight. The sight makes him ache with loss. The last time he'd seen his brother Dov before he'd left for America had been in front of Pearle's horse stalls in the market square, Dov's face pale against a high-collared black Russian shirt that was speckled with spittle from his favorite mare. He'd brought his hand up and stroked her long sad face and the horse nuzzled his hand and whinnied softly, saying her farewell, and Dov had looked at him and nodded without a word, and he'd known it was their farewell also. His brother had grinned at him, the way he did when Yitzhak awakened from a bad dream, as if Dov had been there with him, had ridden in bareback to pull him out of the nightmare.

Keep howling, demons, the teacher tells them. I'll return soon.

But as soon as he leaves, the chanting sputters and stops. Yitzhak finishes the section he is reading silently, so he won't be teased, and brings the pages of the *siddur*, the prayer book, up to his lips. Through the window, he sees Gedalie Ali and Pearle, talking and gesturing, the teacher pacing. *Gimmel, gamel, the hump of the camel.*

Is that his hairy little tokuss? Herschel taunts, standing up next to him. Yitzhak can feel the other boys stir, their eyes glittering in the dark. He looks back down at the *siddur.*

Herschel draws back his foot and kicks Yitzhak lightly in the shin. Again. Again. Harder. The point of pain grows wider, spreads, burns up his leg. He tries to ignore it and concentrate on the Hebrew lines in front of him. *Baruch ataw adonoy elohanu melach haoloam shay motzay lechem min ha-aretz.* Blessed be you, O Lord our God King of the Universe who has brought bread from the earth. Dough from the land of dough. Yitzhak giggles. Herschel's face twitches and he kicks harder— Don't just sit there, lickspittle, get up and run, run away like your toeless brother. How did he run, lickspittle?

Dov chopped off his toes
because of his nose
But still he goes
Run, golem, run

Herschel recites with no problem now, hovering above Yitzhak, the whole coarse, intruding world gathered into his bloated shape, pressing in, hurting. Yitzhak swings the prayer book at it. A corner of the cover slams into Herschel's forehead, just above his eyes. Herschel's forehead blossoms. Yah, yah, he screams.

Yitzhak brings the book back again and starts to swing. A hand grabs his wrist, holds it tightly.

The disappointment in Gedalie Ali's eyes pierces him.

Is this a Jew?

Yitzhak stammers: He said, he called...

He said, he called. And you struck. The world wants our blood and so you draw it for them. As if your brother never left you.

Gedalie Ali takes out his handkerchief, dabs at Herschel's forehead until the bleeding stops. Herschel sobs dramatically. Stop pissing with your eyes, the dwarf says. Enough. He turns to the room. Enough from all of you for now, he says more loudly. Dissolve, clots: go. Nu, what are you waiting for—go. Go, and listen to me now, children, go straight to your houses and go carefully. Don't stray and don't play—this isn't the day for it.

The boys all around Yitzhak rise, buzzing happily at the unexpected holiday. You also, the teacher says to Herschel. Go. Rise, harden, crumble. Live out your cycle.

The room empties. Through the open door, Yitzhak can see the grass burning with light, the boys dark whirling specks against the dazzle, tumbling in the weedy yard in front of the *cheder*.

Gedalie Ali goes out and gestures at him to follow. Come, child, I need to chop some wood.

They walk around the side of the building. The wood is stacked against the wall; an ax leans next to the pile.

He said, he called, the teacher repeats finally. And you hit. What did he say to you about your fiery brother?

Nothing, teacher, Yitzhak says.

I've heard his chant before, child. Gedalie Ali shakes his head. Listen and I'll tell you something because you are the brother of your brother, because you have his fire. Because you hit. I'll tell you what he came to understand. The hatred in your heart can become a golem, a monster in the world. A monster that can turn on us and kill us.

The teacher suddenly looks very tired. He presses his fingers to the sides of his head.

Do you understand? No? Listen. Do you know the story of Rabbi Loew, child?

In Prague, Yitzhak mumbles, looking down. He made a cre-cre- creature...

In Prague he made a cre-cre-creature, Gedalie Ali says. In Prague when the Jews were threatened and killed as we are in this world, Rabbi Loew took clay and fashioned it over the bones of the martyred dead into the shape of a huge man, and with his own fingers, like this—Gedalie Ali writes in the air—can you see him, Yitzhak? the teacher says, his eyes shadowed under his thick, tangled eyebrows, the jutting bones of his forehead echoing, strangely, the ridge of hump on his bowed little back—can you see how with his fingers, their tips burning with anger, he wrote the word *emet*, truth, in the clay of the creature's forehead and he breathed the heat of his heart into the clay mouth and then life pushed veins under the clay. That night the golem rose, and that night and every night it went out into the streets of Prague and killed the killers of the Jews, broke their bones, sealed off the breath in their throats. Until one day it killed without the rabbi telling it to, and the rabbi was afraid that he could no longer control the creature, that the living clay would harm the innocent. That it would bring the vengeance of the gentiles down on our heads. He understood, you see, that we survive by moving between the raindrops, child, by the magic of invisibility and weightlessness. Do you know what he did then? No? It was simple, child. Gedalie Ali squats and draws the word *emet,* truth, in the dust with his finger. אמ/ת. He turned truth into death. So. The dwarf rubs away the *aleph,* leaves *met,* death in the dust. מת. Truth into death. That simple. He destroyed the creature he'd created to be our protector and avenger. But it was necessary. It was simply necessary. There was nothing else to do. The cre-cre-creature had to go.

Run, golem, run.

Gedalie Ali squints at him. Do you understand my story, child? No? Never mind; your brother did—that's what's important. It's all right. I'll put the words here, later they'll hatch.

The spatulate forefinger moves to Yitzhak's forehead, its warmth pulsing into his head.

Go now, child; I'm tired and you drink me like a cup.

He picks up the ax and turns his back on Yitzhak. The ax is nearly his size but he handles it as if it is light as a match stick. Yitzhak stares at the hands wrapped around the haft, the reddened knuckles misshapen and bulbous, the muscle cords under the arm fur twitching and sliding. The bobbing hump on the dwarf's back seems suddenly to hold another, evil brain, driving the powerful arms with maniacal fury. Gedalie Ali raises the ax over the white ax wedge of his face, his expression fierce under his bristling, coarse eyebrows, a changeling hatched into the world. *Gimmel, gamel, golem.*

It begins to rain. Yitzhak watches a light wedge-shaped slash in a log soak and darken. Gedalie Ali's words merge into the words he'd heard between Dov and his father the night before Dov left, the murmur of their voices awakening him. He'd crept to the landing, the way he always did, and he could see the two of them in Papa's room, his brother standing near the large horsehair chair. He'd felt a flutter of fear—only travelers came to that chair: Papa would light a candle, hold it to their faces and peer into their eyes as if to see something inside their heads, a *trachoma*, a quality they must have if they would pass to America. He'd listened to them, straining to understand the mysterious prayer-language of adults, the sing-song of passages and commentaries whose meanings danced like motes of dust just outside his understanding, yet sifted into his memory so he could recite, word for word, as he would *Gemara*, a dialogue of rabbis:

And Dov said: What do you expect to see if you look into my eyes with your light, papa?

And Papa said: Your soul.

And Dov said: How mystical—I thought you searched only for trachoma.

And Papa said: The eye is like an egg; when I put light to it, I see the soul curled inside its cavity. I see it uncurl and move along paths of possibility. Why do you smile?

And Dov said: I see why they pay you. How does it look, papa? The soul?

And Papa said: How do you think? A soft, red, transluctantly luminous sac, as fine-veined as the fetus I once saw ripped from the belly of a Jewish girl by a drunken Russian. Sit.

And Dov sat, his back stiff, his hands gripping the armrests.

And Papa lit the candle and seized Dov's wrist and brought the candle closer with his other hand.

And Dov said: So, nu, can my eyes stand the light of America?—are they focused enough so all they'd will see would be dollars? You're the one who should go—the Jews' benches in that land are only for the Negroes. You could have gone to university, been a physician there, instead of a smuggler. Instead of a dealer in trachoma certificates for would-be travelers.

And Papa said: If the queen had balls. If Jews were gentiles. But we're not, are we?

And Dov said: We can only try.

And Papa said: Is that what you're doing?

And Dov said: What exactly do you see in my eyes, papa?

And Papa said: A dark flow. Blood and flames. Something loosening and releasing terrible things upon us.

And Dov said: What's loose is already loose in the world. So you know. Is that why you have me in this chair? Is that why you want me to leave? In Vilna last week, gentiles melted the candelabra of the synagogue and poured it down the rabbi's throat, saying he was known for his silver tongue. Polish wit. You tell me about a Russian birth; I tell you about a Polish insemination. If you wish, I have more stories.

And Papa said: A terrible story doesn't free you to do terrible things.

And Dov said: It gives them the license of example to exist. It loosens them into life.

And Papa stared into Dov's eyes and said: Like a golem?

And Dov said: So you know that too.

And Papa said: I'm not alone in that knowledge. Golem...how mystical. I thought your organization searched only for earthly solutions.

And Dov said: We regard it as an accurate metaphor. The golem was a construct, a creature of the anger in our hearts, an instrument of terror against those who terrorized us. Terror against terror.

And Papa said: Examine that metaphor. Once loosened, the golem couldn't be bridled. The creator became the creature of his creature.

And Dov looked down and said: The golem was a limited strategic action. A means to an end. When its goal was met, it was discontinued. Just like that. And if it gets out of control, so what? The task of terror is to set chaos into motion, to let a terrible situation spin out of control. In other words, what do we lose? Lives? Lives will be lost anyway, one way or another.

And Papa said: Whose words are you reciting to convince yourself? You know what will be lost, heart. I can see into you. Your eyes blink and I'm taken and carried by a dream that blows into my head like a dark wind. Darkness moving softly into darkness.

And for a moment Dov said nothing. And closed his eyes.

And said: Are you worried about my soul or everybody else's ass?

And said: I have a new wife with a child in her womb.

And Papa said: Sarah will stay with her parents in Lomza until you can send for her; I've spoken to them.

And Dov said: Papa, I don't know what to do. I cut off my toes so I wouldn't have to kill. So I could stay here. Now I have to sever myself from myself.

And Papa said: Hazak v'et hazak. Strength and more strength.

Gedalie Ali's ax swings down. Yitzhak sees his brother holding his bare foot against a stump, his face intent, the identical arc, the toes flying like bullets. *I liberated them from my foot, little one, in order to liberate myself.* He'd freed himself, but now he'd had to run anyway, run without toes.

Papa brought the flame closer.

Run golem run.

What would his father see if he looked into his eyes? What did the dwarf see? Yitzhak suddenly knows the truth, *emet*, written on his own forehead, knows what Gedalie Ali had been trying to tell him, knows he's his brother's brother, understands the passage now, knows what he has to do. He closes his eyes. The candle flame still flickers behind his lids. He stares at the small bright twist, the little skullish face at its blue center, the candlelight licking its dark sockets. The face swells out of the light, rises to his kiss: clay flesh cracked to expose white skullbone, black Hebrew letters gouged into the forehead, clawed down around the deep blood-welled eye-sockets, the curved grin of broken teeth outlined and stained with red mud, the forehead engraved with truth, *emet*, אמת, the letter *aleph*, א, he must erase to create death, to kill the killer in his heart.

Now I have to sever myself from myself.

Hazak v'et hazak.

The ax rises, begins to fall. He rushes forward, brushes by Gedalie Ali's legs, sticks his hand, the hand that struck at Herschel, the golem's hand, onto the wet wood altar waiting under the fall of the arc. A part of him that sees the way his soul sees the dream now sees the dwarf twisting the ax desperately, the sharp edge turning away, up, but the arc completes itself, down, a bone-grinding grip seizes and thrusts his hand into the candle flame and it sears up through his veins and bursts behind his eyes and he stretches and flickers long and thin and impossibly thin and out.

And comes back, slowly. A drifting dust of letters gathering on an empty page. Lying in a thick silence. In blackness. In rain. In mud. He hears the sound of his own breathing in it and he knows he has breath. He hears breathing over him and a warm spot of breath touches his face and he knows he has flesh. The pain pulses in his hand like a heart, and he knows he has flesh.

He feels himself gripped, pulled up embraced against a hard, warm chest.

He opens his eyes and sees Gedalie Ali's stricken face, his hairy cheeks streaked with mud or blood or rain or tears. I know, I know, the dwarf is saying, rocking him. Shah, it's all right, my light, I know, and Yitzhak feels his teacher gently writing the letters that will bring him to life or death on the cool smoothness of his forehead.

AIRPORT

"Over three million Jews died in the Nazi death camps on Polish soil. Tens of thousands were saved by their fellow citizens—Poles who risked their lives in order to give them shelter. It should be borne in mind that Poland was the only country where death at the hands of the Nazis was the punishment for aiding Jews."

from The Judaics of Poland
published by Orbis—the government tourist agency

In sitting down to type my handwritten draft into the computer, I noticed that my first line for this section read: "I returned to Kolno during the same month— July—that its Jewish community was destroyed some fifty years before." The line is not only awkward, but also, of course, inaccurate: I couldn't return to a place I'd never been. But the sentence still struck me as a good example of the Rorschach quality of language— inaccurate words reflecting, accurately, an emotion—an accidental truth.

The date of my trip was accidental also. I'd made my travel plans to coincide with my return from Boston, and it wasn't until I'd read the Kolno memorial book that I realized the significance of the month I'd picked. I was in London with my family during the first week of July, and I left my wife and son there and flew to Brussels to catch a connecting flight into Warsaw. I hadn't felt it when we'd left the States, but taking off from Heathrow, alone, I felt suddenly as if I was twisting off the stem of my life. My existence was all an illusion, some writer's dream: my parents had never left Kolno; I'd been born and died there, my head smashed against the stones of the market square.

It had been a long time since I'd been to Europe, and flying over the green Belgian countryside, I was struck by the utter reasonableness of the landscape: perfectly square groves of trees planted in symmetrical rows, each evenly spaced from the other and placed intelligently between the precise green and yellow squares of the fields. "Yet this too was once part of the darkness," Conrad said—but from the air the continent seemed as clipped and controlled as a mowed lawn. Brussels, the signs in the airport told me, was where Europe did business. The airport waiting lounges had the contained feel of a mall and without the ticket and reservation counters in fact could have been one: bright and shiny and Euro-chic, its stores full of stylishly displayed rows of soft leather handbags and briefcases and luggage, glinting bottles of perfume and cologne, bouquets of pastel colored scarves and ties, gleaming loops of silver bracelets and necklaces. Passengers roamed between the shops and the airline counters dressed in the same styles and carrying the same luggage and briefcases displayed behind the windows so that their reflections on the glass seemed tangled in the displays.

My stomach had been tied up in knots since I'd boarded the plane in Heathrow. When I went in to use the toilet and shut the stall door I noticed, with some leap of anarchistic glee, that the inside of the door had been desecrated with graffiti, smudged names and comments, which more often than not simply consisted of the names of countries: Mali, Guinea, Kenya, Malaysia, Pakistan: "Soe Lein from Burma." Linking and separating the names and countries like some verbal UN peacekeeping force was the universal English obscenity, sometimes illustrated with unlikely genitalia. There was a subversive, underground quality about the scrawls and scratches here, a silent murmur of rebellion against the creepy homogenization of the airport and the landscape. I remembered that Bruce Weigl was coming to Brussels next month for a conference: I though he'd understand this door. I remembered how he had been taken by the film *Jacob's Ladder*: he was sure it was a secret biography of his life. Maybe he'd sit here. "Weigl," I wrote on the inside of the door, "We're on the Ladder."

The waiting area for the flight to Poland was in a distant corridor of the airport, far from the trendy cafes and duty free shops: one had to take three different moving walkways to get to it. Many of the Poles waiting patiently in the hard plastic chairs—all flights were delayed because of a controllers' slow down strike—looked slightly off also—in clothing, in haircuts, in shoes, in body language—from the Euro-Mall ideal. Slightly off, but trying hard, and only one of them met the expectations of stereotype so exactly he'd moved into that state of unselfconsciousness that allowed him to become a parody of a parody: a hard-faced, raw knuckled fiftyish man with a stiff gray brush-back Wolfman haircut and a jeans leisure suit, its seams glittering with rows of silver studs, a wild-and-crazy-guy red pointed collar pressed flat around his jacket lapels. I liked him immediately in the same way I liked the subversive graffiti I'd seen on the toilet stall door. Like all the others, he carried a basket full of presents, loot carried back to the hinterland. Moving into their waiting area, I felt myself crossing a line.

I had a row of three seats for myself on the flight. The woman across the aisle from me had a baby in a carrier; when she ate lunch she put both into the aisle. The Belgium stewardess, stepping around the child, looked at her sternly. Madame, she said, you are inconveniencing everybody. The stewardesses on this flight had all seemed unsmiling, brusque and authoritative with the passengers—I didn't know if it was the accepted style on Sabena or simply snobbery towards these country cousins from the poorer East. I did something I would never do in the States or England, but that would have been a natural action, reaction, in Israel—I picked up the child and held it for a while. The mother smiled at me and said something in Polish. I shook my head and smiled back. "You're not Polish?" she said to me, in English, in surprise.

What did she recognize in me? I couldn't look at her face without picturing it in Kolno, at the market square. I remembered what the Orbis guide book on Jewish life in Poland the embassy in Washington had sent me stated, rather defensively, I'd thought, about Poles saving Jewish lives in spite of Poland being the only country in Europe where helping the Jews meant the death penalty. Would this woman's face have been twisted with hate or glee that the upstart Jews, the foreigners in their midst who laughed secretly when good Christians went by, who owned the town but couldn't, or wouldn't even speak decent Polish, were finally getting their payback? Or perhaps she would have been someone like Tsesha Kosskowski, one of the people I'd read about in the Kolno book: she had stopped Rachel Alter-Borkowski, a Kolno Jew who came back after the war and told her, in deep shame, what her neighbors had done to the Jews—and then told Borkowski how her husband, a church-organist tried to hide some Jews but was denounced by others and shot by the Germans. Or Halina Golshovska-Glaser, another Pole, who brought a bottle of water to a Jew squeezed into one of the lorries at the market-square and was slapped so hard by a German that she nearly fainted.

I gave the child back and looked out of the window, watching the fields of Germany and then of Poland being brushed by the shadow of the wing. I tried to feel something. I pulled the curtain down and tried to read. Besides the Kolno book, the Orbis book and a guide to Poland, I'd brought four books that seemed appropriate along with me on the trip, though when I looked at them again, I wondered what else my definition of appropriate might include—I had taken along the reading list for the perfect Jewish neurotic's holiday, a literal guilt trip. Three of them—though this hadn't, at least consciously, been the reason for my choice—were by writers who had committed suicide: Primo Levi's *The Drowned and the Saved*, and *The Survivor* and *Writing into the World* by Terrance Des Pres, the young Colgate Holocaust scholar who'd died in 1987. The fourth was *Four Hours in My Lai* by Michael Bilton and Kevin Sim. During the flight and the time I was in Poland, I found it impossible to read straight through any of these: I found myself reading a paragraph or a page or two in one, then picking up another and doing the same. The words and the images they formed merged in my mind and mingled under what I was seeing and feeling in another kind of nightmarish Talmudic commentary.

THE MARKET SQUARE

❖

Kolno was in that part of Poland taken by the Soviet Union under the Hitler-Stalin pact of 1939. The Jews of the town—the majority of its citizens—were for the most part rendered destitute and desperate under the Soviets, who categorized the town's tradesmen and craftsmen as unproductive elements, tore down the stalls and stores of the market square and made it into a public park, complete with a statue of Lenin. As a result, of course, most of the Jews of Kolno became unemployed. Bundists, Zionists, and finally even the local Jewish communists who helped the Soviets administer the area, were arrested and deported, either to inner Russia or to slave labor camps in the Gulag: they turned out to be the lucky ones. Eventually the community, as it always did, began adapting. "Antels"— labor battalions of tailors, bakers, shoemakers and carpenters were established, and Jews got work digging the trench fortifications being dug between the town and the East Prussian border.

The trenches proved to be a mini-Maginot line. On the evening of July 22, 1941, while many of the Red Army soldiers were at a party with local political sympathizers, German paratroopers landed, annihilated frontier patrols and secured strategic points around the town. Kolno was bombarded and swiftly occupied.

Life immediately went from bad to hellish for the Jews. They were made to suffer random humiliations and murders both at the hands of both the Germans and their Polish neighbors who, in the words of Dinah Koncepolsky-Chludniewitz, the only Jewish survivor of the Nazi occupation of Kolno, along with "Russian bootlickers,"

> ...did everything in their power to get in the good graces of the Nazi authorities. These Christian traitors did not sell their lives to the Nazis for thirty shekels of silver, but rated a Jew's life at the price of half a pound of salt and some were even satisfied by a Nazi's smile or a shoulder pat...Poles gaily robbed and murdered their neighbors in full view of the Nazis... Ya'kov Zabilowitz and the elderly Bramson were forced to undress and were brutally beaten to death to the tune of mocking shouts and laughter; Chaim Gross and Moshe Merachek, the blacksmith, were shot by German gendarmes in the middle of the street...

On the fourth of July, only two weeks after the occupation, the final events that marked the end of the Jewish community in Kolno began. When the Germans had first come to the town, some of the Poles, seeking to gain favor, tried to demolish the statue of Lenin. On the fourth, a Friday, the Polish police passed an on an order from the Germans: all Jews in the area were to report to the former market square; craftsmen were to bring their tools. Under German guns and whips, the Jews were forced to demolish the statue of Lenin with their tools—or with bare hands—-and load the rubble into two carts, while "the Poles stood there—men and women, old men and youths, their faces inflamed and excited—cursing loudly and making fun of the toiling and tortured Jews." Koncepolsky-Chludniewitz could only find a comparison for the event by recalling Jewish history: "It was a terrible scene," she recounts, "which reminded me of the Spanish Inquisition." Some Jews were given whips and told to lash others: if they beat too gently, they were lashed themselves. Several Jews were then harnessed to the carts and made to pull them, filled with the statue's rubble, to the Jewish cemetery while the others were forced to form a procession and sing and weep as if at a funeral. At the cemetery they were made to dig a grave and bury the rubble while singing:

> *Because of the Jew*
> *The war came to you*
> *But golden Hitler arrived*
> *And made him work*

When "Lenin's funeral" was over, the Germans and Poles left the Jews standing in the cemetery. It was almost curfew time—any Jew found on the street would be shot—and so the people raced for their homes. There was no safety to be found though: whatever had been unleashed at the market square was now alive in the town. When darkness came the Poles staged a pogrom, raping, robbing and murdering: Koncepolsky-Chludniewitz recalls: "My cousin, Deborah Dudowitz, the Brismans and the Dolowitch family...were among the victims. The two Dolowitch daughters had been raped and then killed" Fifteen families were murdered that night.

The next day the Germans burned the Torahs and prayer books in the synagogue, and in the following weeks tormented the community with random shootings, beatings, forced labors and decrees: Jews had to wear yellow patches, Jews could no longer walk on the pavements but only in the middle of the street. When it became too dangerous to go to the synagogue, they prayed in the cellar of Guta-Leah's house. Reading that description, I thought of Koncepolsky-Chludniewitz's comparison with the Inquisition, and I wondered if that historical model had been in their minds: there was always a precedent of suffering and survival in Jewish history. They would pray the way the Marranos had prayed: they would suffer, but they would do their best to survive as Jews and then the pogrom would be over and a precarious sanity would return—or those that did survive would leave. They had thought everything that could be done to them as a people had already been done.

"On the 15th of July," Koncepolsky-Chludniewitz remembered, "the Germans commanded all the men, aged 16 and above, to gather in the market square and bring food for one day with them, as they would be going out to work." When they arrived, the men were loaded into and then driven away in four lorries to the defensive trenches many of them must have helped dig. They were never seen again, though "After some days the Poles were heard to say that the ground in the trenches...had been seen shaking and trembling." Three days later the parents and wives and children of the murdered men were told to report to the market square with luggage and valuables. They were loaded onto the same trucks and driven to the nearby village of Meschtshevoye, near Stavisk, where they were machine-gunned into a mass grave. The third action took place at the end of July when all the remaining Jews were ordered to the market square. From the descriptions, what happened must have been a combination of a Polish pogrom and the more orderly murder the Germans preferred. The Polish mob, eager to prove itself to the Germans, attacked the Jews gathered there. Babies were torn from their mother's arms and their brains dashed out on the stones: people who tried to run away or to resist and were shot on the spot. The women and children were taken by lorry to Meschtshevoye and machine gunned. The men were made to walk to Kolimagi and machine gunned into ditches there.

Perhaps fifty Jews tried to run away from the town when they'd received the order to go to the market square, but most of them were caught and turned over to the Germans by Polish farmers. It was death for any Pole to harbor Jews, as the Orbis guide told me, but not every farmer was deterred by this policy. Koncepolsky-Chludniewitz and a friend escaped and were hidden by Michael Tcharnetzki, a farmer who'd been a friend of her family. She survived the war (though her friend didn't) by posing as a Polish worker—she ended up working in Germany. There were only two other immediate survivors of the final exterminations. A man named Bocka Eidenberg and a woman named Chaya-Leah Olech had run away and taken refuge in a barn. When the farmer found them sleeping in his hay in the morning, he got a German policeman, who arrested the two, put them into a cart and started to take them, with the farmer's help, to the police station. Along the way, somehow Eidenberg got his hands loose: he grabbed the policeman and while he was choking him, Chaya-Leah drew out the man's dagger and stabbed him to death. The farmer managed to run away. The couple, hunted, a price on their heads, hid in the forest until 1944, when the Germans found and killed them. Besides Koncepolsky-Chludniewitz, none of the other Kolno Jews who were there during those end days in the market-square survived the war.

In the three actions that occurred from the beginning of July 1941 to the beginning of August, all the other Jews of Kolno, over two thousand people, were murdered. Halina Golshovska-Glaser, one of the Kolno Poles who'd been horrified by the events in her town, wrote to a Jewish friend:

Dear friend, no ghetto was established in Kolno. The town was too small so the Germans murdered all the Jews in a very short time. When they had collected them all in the marketplace, they loaded their luggage onto special lorries: the men in one group, the women and children in another, and were sent in two directions—to Meschtshevoye and to the other side of Zabiele, where the antitank trenches and special ditches had been dug. The Jews were ordered to undress and were machine-gunned. All of them—those who fell dead together with the wounded and unhurt— were heaped into the trenches. People who witnessed all this can tell that for three days the earth there was seen to quiver and tremble.

RUMORS: FLOW

Something is coming, its breath or the anticipation of its breath blowing people away. The village seems to be emptying around my mother, as if it is in the final moments of a dream from which she will shortly awake. Jews disappear. First it is the poor: the market-square beggars, the fixers, wood cutters, bristle makers and tanners who lived in the dank wooden hovels and tangles of dark alleys near the cemetery. Then those with more to leave behind. One day they are home, people my mother has known all her life, the next day they are gone, their houses empty. The shape of the world melts. One day she wakes up and her brother Dov is gone. The next day her little brother Yitzhak is brought home draped over the humpback of his teacher, the dwarf Gedalie Ali. In the doorway they look like the photograph of Siamese twins she's seen. Chang and Eng. Two legs, four arms, two heads. Her brother and Gedalie Ali are sealed together with blood. Teacher and pupil. My grandmother, Sarah Gittel, screams but then falls silent. A strange birth, she mutters, her eyes going distant, as Gedalie Ali peels Yitzhak from his back and lays him on the horsehair couch. Yitzhak's hand is shattered and bloody, his face swollen and bruised. Blood calls to blood, Gedalie Ali says. The world's unknitting. Beware.

Yasha, the Polish maid who had been her wet nurse, vanishes from her life also, though her father, my grandfather Pinhas, tells her Yasha's still in Kolno, afraid to work for them. Invisible borders have trenched through the town. Sarah Gittel refuses to clean. My mother tries to hold the house together but the furniture is always so furry with dust it seems to her the tables and chairs are blurring into the air. She finds plates with scraps of rotting meat left to stink in the halls. A spot of green mold on the ceiling becomes a continent. Her father's face is stamped with worry. One moment Sarah Gittel berates him for not forcing them to flee with Dov to America, the next she curses him for worrying her with his precautions, the cave-like space he's dug out under the floorboards, secretly carting the dirt off to the forest during the night.

Why should we disappear into a hole—we've done nothing. What's coming for us?

He laughs bitterly. The century, he says. My mother joins nervously and involuntarily in his laughter; she doesn't find what he says funny but she's never heard her father laugh like this. Sarah Gittel glares at her. At that very moment, her body, for the first time, begins to bleed. She feels herself flowing away. Mama, she calls. She reaches under her skirt, draws back red fingers. The entire house begins to tremble and shift. Dust demons rise and dance before her eyes. Yitzhak moans from his sick bed. Do you see what you did? Sarah Gittel screams at her. Outside she hears the crack of a hundred thunderclaps and instantly an echoing crack appears in the wall. Books fall from the shelves. Here it is now, her father mutters. She bursts into tears. Her mother turns and slaps her so hard her ears ring. Now cry, *pickholtz*, simpleton. See if the goyim won't come because you weep.

A series of explosions shakes the house again. Glass falls from the windows facing the market square. Between the stalls, a girl, my mother's friend Miriam Weiss, runs by, chased by a group of laughing Poles, their faces streaked with dirt and blood, as if they'd been released from the earth when the bombs fell. Through the windows my mother sees them run from one frame to the other as if passing into a series of pictures hung in her mind. Sarah Gittel pulls the curtains shut, stares at her with hatred, as if holding her responsible. Quickly, little fool, bring the food, the water; help for once, help with your brother. There's no time for your nonsense now.

In the darkness under their floor, they sit, necks bent, among the sacks of potatoes that her father had lugged down, along with Yitzhak's mattress. In his hands, he holds the green ledger that contains a record of his business transactions.

We'll eat that last, Sarah Gittel says.

What were you doing upstairs? I thought you were going to bring down more of the food and blankets. And the water—we only have one jug. Armies clash above our heads; who knows how long we'll have to burrow here.

Is it a wife's job to think of such things? Sarah Gittel says. Did I bury us here? She lights a candle and glances at her daughter, a look full of blame. What's come from me? her daughter asked Sarah Gittel when she'd drawn her into the bedroom to staunch her flow. The sin of Eve, Sarah Gittel had said, wadding linen. The Lord punished her for wanting to take his Power by giving it to her. Now you're so blessed also. Mazel Tov. Say nothing to your father.

More explosions shake the house. Dust falls from the walls, coating their flesh. My mother—for the rest of her life she'll be claustrophobic, so that even in the seeping away of her consciousness during her last days she'll scream for the door to her room to be left open—feels the floor above her head press in on her: the space is too shallow for any of them to stand up.

You've buried us before we're dead, Sarah Gittel says to her husband.

We'll be safe here.

We'll grow like potatoes with our heads in the earth.

My mother sits perfectly still in the semidarkness, her flesh trembling with the walls. She feels sick with power. Yitzhak cries and moans. His head is hot as a stove. But she won't cry. She won't let any more of her body drain out and become things in the world.

A day, a night, another day, another night. They huddle in the darkness. Shrieks pierce through the thick walls; at times they hear footsteps thudding over their heads. Her father takes the ax he uses to chop wood and sits with it across his lap. Worse than the footsteps is the scurrying and scratching all around her. Warm hairy bodies scamper across her legs. When she starts to scream, Sarah Gittel clamps a hand over her mouth, whispers in her ear. Be quiet, they're just fellow hiders in the darkness. Keep them from your brother. My mother curls her body around Yitzhak's head, flailing her arms or kicking whenever the rats get close. The water is gone. In the darkness they feel themselves losing first time, then form, so every once in a while Sarah Gittel must light a candle to bring them back to themselves. Their lips swell and crack. When my mother swallows, she feels her swollen throat constrict painfully around a thin sharp shard of dry bone. Yitzhak has stopped moaning. When she brings her face close to his in the darkness, his breath is cold and rank, the last trapped breath in the mouth of a corpse. He stares blankly. Mama, she croaks. Sarah Gittel lights a candle and looks at her son. She picks up the chamber pot and carries it to Yitzhak. Cradling his face in her lap, she fills a small cup, pours it into his cracked lips. The stench intensifies in the air. The urine dribbles over his lips, down his chin. My mother sees his throat constricting. Sarah Gittel drinks next, gestures to her daughter, her husband. It's only us, she says. The candle light flickers against the walls. My mother sees in it the flame of her mother's anger, pushing out, holding the walls firm against the world.

What kind of time do potatoes know, growing with their heads in the earth? She's no longer sure how many days have passed in the world of day and night. Sometimes moans and whispers penetrate the thick walls as if they've become thin as membrane. Wisps of smoke drift through invisible cracks. A thick acrid stink fills the air. Her father rocks in prayer. She watches her mother looking at him with a contempt she suddenly understands. She hears shots, a series of thuds against the walls of the house, the clomp of footsteps.

Don't worry; they'll have to chop through the floor to get to us, her father whispers.

The goyim don't have axes? Sarah Gittel asks.

Yitzhak moans. The noise stops. It doesn't matter, Sarah Gittel says. Soon we'll dry up and blow away like dust. She lights the candle, picks up the chamber pot, shakes it tiredly so they can see it's empty, dry. They have nothing left to piss into it.

He's dying, she says. We're dying, dried and husked as if caught in webs.

Pinhas, gripping the ax, crawls across to the wall on the market square side of the house. He and Sarah Gittel stare at each other, then he turns from her gaze and begins to hit the blunt end of the ax head against the plaster wall. Sarah Gittel lights the candle. A patch of red appears as the plaster falls; my mother sees the outlines of bricks that looks lighter, cleaner than the rest of the wall.

He slams the ax against the bricks until they crack and fall apart, then pulls out the pieces. My mother sees a white cataract, glowing over the hole. Her father reverses the ax and smashes the handle end against the whiteness. The ice cracks and suddenly his face is pale and thin in the moonlight and she can see the preserved world outside, held between white teeth. He reaches into the opening. Sarah Gittel blows out the candle and crawls next to him. He hands her a shard of ice; she sucks it greedily. He reaches cautiously outside, scoops in a handful of dripping snow. Come, Sarah Gittel whispers to mother, come help me take some to your brother.

My mother hears a scraping noise and turns quickly. Yitzhak, his bandaged hand bleeding, his face white, has risen to his hands and knees and is staring at the glowing white sphere that her father opened in the wall. He begins pulling himself towards it over the dirt floor. Yitzhak, she whispers, get back. But Sarah Gittel smiles at him, nods. Come, come to moisture, to light. Come, *kaddish*, her father says, come to life, come, Ruhu. Yitzhak inches towards the opening. My mother crawls beside him so they arrive at the hole the same time. They wrap their arms around each other. Entwined they peer through the blind, cracked eye. Chang and Eng. They both push their heads against the opening as if suckling together. They stick their tongues out and lick at the icy liquid. They reach out and stuff snow into their mouths. The cold lump melts slowly in my mother's mouth, its released moisture softening the dry, cracked membranes of her tongue, seeping coldly and deliciously down her throat, numbing her lips. She looks through the hole. Here are the cobblestones of the street, shining under a rime of ice, the market square across it held by the jagged rat teeth of ice at the top and a clean lip of snow at the bottom, nimbused in a halo as if it has just been created. She licks the snow. As her eyes hunt, she sees the cracked world born from her body. Tongues of flame lick the sky behind the market square and in the square the stall of Lisbin, the kosher butcher is burning. For an instant she thinks she sees the form of the butcher himself, hanging in his stall like a side of meat. Other shapes are scattered on the ground like broken dolls.

Strange figures suddenly run into the street, weaving and ducking in a grotesque dance. They scream silently, smoke pouring from their nostrils, faces distorted and blackening. Purim, Yitzhak whispers, his flesh shivering against hers.

She stares. Framed by a glowing halo of whiteness, the very mouth of astonishment, the figures outside dance in the snow and fall into twisted postures and attitudes, like strange black letters written against the snow. A young man on a white horse rides by out of a miracle. He suddenly throws up his hands, clutches his breast and falls into the street, his eyes locked to hers, rolling like a horse's eyes. Yitzhak trembles with silent laughter. Blood gouts from the young man; it gushes magically through the gutter to her window, blood to blood. She reaches her fingers out into the warm stream and brings them back to her lips, connects herself to the flow of the world.

WARSAW

Warsaw was the man in the denim leisure suit: rough-skinned and raw-knuckled but trying to dress towards a model that was still a little fuzzy in his head, something perhaps glimpsed on a TV screen behind a shop window as he strolled past. Not far from the central train station was a more convenient metaphor, the 42-story (former) Palace of Culture, a grotesque Stalinist era skyscraper that looked like a clumsy attempt to create a counter-image to the capitalist Empire State building, its cornices topped with tacky squiggles and spires, its facade streaked and dirty: it had been turned, the taxi driver who brought me from the airport told me proudly, into a gambling casino. I'd booked a room in the Holiday Inn: the price was good and the reservation had been easy to make from England, but as I checked in I wondered how much of my motivation was simply to have a safe haven—a familiar cocoon of soft carpeting, elevators with brass doors and framed iconic photographs of elaborate, impossible meals bolted to their walls—that I could step back into and away from whatever I'd find here. Most of the other guests appeared to be Japanese businessmen looking for economic opportunities in the opening Eastern bloc. They weren't the only ones: the taxi driver asked me if I'd be interested in meeting "Soviet girls." They were desperate in Russia, he said, grinning happily; they were pouring into Warsaw now. Reagan, he said, and winked at me.

That afternoon I walked from the hotel to the area where the Warsaw ghetto had been. It was about a mile walk, though in actuality the place where the hotel was located would have been included in the initial ghetto area that the Germans decreed in November of 1940— at that time Jews made up a third of the city's population, 380,000 people, and the ghetto was filled with over half a million as Jews from outside Warsaw were packed inside its walls. The map of the ghetto in the Orbis book is like a diagram of a shrinking amoeba—in 1940 a huge nebulous shape is super-imposed over the gridwork of streets, its head butting the pitchfork prongs of the railway tracks, then a straight red line divides it in half in August 1942, as its population depletes due to starvation and disease and the deportations to the Treblinka extermination camp. Finally there is only a small shaded area at the top of the amoeba, perhaps a fifth of the original: this is the ghetto area from September 1942 to April of 1943, to the end of the revolt.

I walked up Jana Pawla Boulevard, its modern shops and boutiques and restaurants and hotels and offices, marked with Japanese and American corporate logos, a brightly glowing screen in front of streets of drab brown and gray apartment blocks. A Burger King sat across from a kiosk that advertised Golden American 25's: "American Full Flavor—Made in USA." As I looked down the street the word *America* or *American* kept snagging my eye, buried in nearly every sign and advertising slogan like a cabalistic formula. In places the boulevard's new facades gaped into weedy lots set off as bazaars: six by six kiosks of painted plywood stood in rows, as if exhibits of a preliminary, primitive stage of the free market economy, their flap windows raised to display vegetables, utensils, tools, clothing, plastic toys, snacks. A sign on one food stall proclaimed Kiosk Hanoi. Peasant women squatted on the sidewalks or on the grass, selling mushrooms and greens and tomatoes.

The balconied apartment buildings behind the strip looked streaked and worn, but many of the balconies were festooned with satellite dishes. There were beggars on every street corner.

"We can buy anything now," the clerk at the hotel had told me, "but not enough people have enough money." Warsaw reminded me of that blend of Western European prosperity and Eastern European architecture and attitudes that had marked Yugoslavia in the seventies when I'd lived in Belgrade for a time. Maybe the former Yugoslavia, with its hourly inflation rate of two or three percent, its post-communist economic woes triggering and exacerbating the ethnic hatreds that have boiled into a frenzied ritualistic suicide, was the real nightmare being held at bay by the city's fearfully whispered mantra of America, America, America.

A part of me, in a journalistic tic, was trying to make that kind of observation, while another was numb with a heavy awareness that was almost like grief. I wasn't quite sure if I was going the right way, but I was reluctant to ask anyone for directions. I passed a park and I thought how my mother had come here when a girl; she'd played in a park with her brother, remembered him wetting his pants. As on the plane, my head full of the Kolno book, I couldn't look at anything or anyone without wondering what extended back in time from them, how it juxtaposed with my own history. It was the way I had seen the Vietnamese writer Le Minh Khue's face when I'd first met her and the way she had seen mine, the historical and the personal inextricably wrapped: everything I saw now touched and rubbed me as if a new and raw sense had emerged. I thought how in my last fiction and in Le Minh Khue's the image that kept coming up was bones, the bones of the uneasy dead that the living walked over, suddenly unearthed and clamoring for attention.

Armed resistance in the ghetto started when the population had been shrunk by starvation, disease, shootings and deportations to the Treblinka death camp down to 60,000 people. In January of 1943, when the Germans attempted their final roundup, they were met by gunfire and forced to retreat from the ghetto. The fighters were organized under the Jewish Combat

Organization—the ZOB—and were commanded by Mordechai Anielewicz; they had obtained and manufactured weapons and ammo and had built a network of bunkers. On April 19th the Germans again tried to round people up for a final extermination and a full scale uprising began. Over 2,000 German regulars and SS soldiers, supported by tanks and artillery attacked the Ghetto: the ZOB headquarters bunker at Mila 18 fell on May 8th, and organized resistance was over by the middle of that month, though small pockets of fighters were hiding in the ruins, killing Germans until well into July. General Stroop, who commanded the German forces, reported killing 5,565 Jews in combat and capturing 56,065—he executed 7,000 immediately and sent the rest to Treblinka to be killed. The Polish underground estimated 1,400 German casualties. Whatever buildings hadn't been destroyed by the fighting were demolished by the Germans.

Old people stared at me from the dark squares of windows in the surrounding apartment buildings, and a lion pride of fat cats lounged in the sun near the monument to the Revolt, an idealized sculpture of beefy, well-muscled heroic figures striking heroic poses. The large park in front of the statue was mostly empty: a few old people on the benches, a number of card tables and an awning-shaded booth where Poles were selling cheaply printed books on Judaica and the Holocaust. There were no other tourists there. I looked at the monument and looked at some of the books. The people on the benches looked at me. Two tour buses pulled up and the tourists came pouring into the square, the two groups mingling, people taking pictures of the monument and of themselves in front of the monument. One of the groups was German, the other Japanese.

The street bordering the east side of the park is named Mordecai Anielewicz. The street behind the monument, on the northern edge of the park, is Mila. Large balconied apartment buildings and pleasant tree-lined streets cover the ruins. There are playgrounds and shops and people going on with their lives. I thought how there should be something good about that. How can you go around constantly thinking about what's under your feet? But my reaction was unintellectual, illogical, visceral: living here seemed complicity in murder.

I walked along Mila Street. Between a high-rise apartment building and a weedy vacant lot was a small park with a grassy mound in its center, concrete steps going up one side of it. This was the remains of Anielewicz' command bunker. The fighting had been fierce here, with no resistance and no quarter. I remembered seeing a "poem" written, I believe by Anielewicz and displayed at the Yad Vashem Holocaust Memorial in Jerusalem. "Kill them," it said. "With guns, with knives, with bricks, with acid, with your bare hands, with your fingernails, with your teeth." He and his staff had committed suicide here rather than fall into German hands. In the film *Shoah*, a survivor now living in Israel describes haunting the ruins and rubble after the fighting was over, praying for death. "If you licked my heart," he said, "it would poison you."

The command bunker was identified by a sign engraved in Yiddish, Hebrew and Polish. A family of tourists was camped behind the mound in a geodesic shell tent. In the weedy vacant field next to it couples strolled. A young man moved diagonally across the field with a net bag full of groceries dangling from one hand; he was taking a short cut to his apartment. He would enter the dark, cool hall and go up the stairs. The building is getting more rundown; kids have spray-painted the names of American heavy metal groups on the walls. He opens his door and his wife greets him. As he puts away the groceries, she complains about the difficulties they're having stretching their salaries to cover expenses: food prices are going through the ceiling. He looks around at their furniture: the sofa and love seat with a matching floral pattern: he remembers how the salesman told them it had been treated with some sort of chemical to make it resistant to stains, it would last for years, they could just wipe any spills away. They'd dreamt about this set when they were courting, standing hand in hand in front of the display window in the furniture store, as if it was a symbol behind glass of the life they sought. But he feels they've lost some of the sense of hope and excitement they'd had when they at last bought the set and this apartment. Everything looks a little shabby and threadbare now, and he's ashamed of this perception, at his extension of that symbolic moment to encompass the feeling of erosion he's had more and more lately. But looking around he can't even remember how their excitement felt. They wonder if they can afford a child. But then they decide they can't be that calculating about it: they've gotten the apartment, the furniture; they're saving for a car: a child seems inevitable. They have to do something. They repeat this last phrase over and over to each other as they begin to make love, as if they're afraid to let a silence fall.

Stawki Street intersects Mila: it's the street where the railroad station is, the Unschlag-platz where Jews from the ghetto were taken to be put on the trains to Treblinka. There are trolley tracks in the middle of the road. On the side of the road where I was walking was a large, drab building, its walls stained, its windows streaked with dirt. I see a small sign up about ten feet over my head on the side of the wall to my left: it was also in Polish, Yiddish and Hebrew and had the words Treblinka and Umschlag-platz on it. Another sign, nearer to eye level, told me that this building contained the Psychological Testing Center of the University of Warsaw. On the side of the building, inside a little courtyard, young women were lined up in front of a bulletin board, checking test scores.

A little further down and across the street was the monument to the train station: white concrete walls set around a small square, the gap between two of the walls in front forming a doorway, its top bridged by a half-oval of concrete to form a stylized "gateway." On the walls inside were carved 400 Jewish first names, though why these names I wasn't sure, unless they were meant to be representative. 300,000 Jews left from the ramp here, to be killed in Treblinka. People had left *yartzeit* memorial candles and flowers inside. As I looked around, I became aware of a young man, bare-chested under a sleeveless jean jacket, staring at me. It was a stare, it seemed to me, I had been getting from many of the people in this neighborhood, half-apologetic, half-defiant. I stared back, almost eager for confrontation, for him to say something. But he only looked at me, as if in surprise, and walked away. I wondered if what I was seeing in people's faces were only reflections of my own mood.

Maybe not. At night I walked to the synagogue near my hotel. It was the only surviving synagogue in Warsaw: it survived because the Germans had used it as a stable and American Jews had donated money to restore it after the war. It was now a handsome two-story stone building with large arched stained-glass windows. The walls of the buildings and advertising cylinders near it were looped and filigreed with graffiti, some of it Jewish Kilroy was here: Stars of David, statements in English and Hebrew: I am here, we are here. I felt that the word "still" was missing from the statements. The other graffiti, more numerous, included swastikas, Heil Hitlers, *Kill the Jews*, *Skins Rule*, and even *White Power*, written in English. We are here. Still. I didn't understand the Polish graffiti, except for the word "Zydowski," Jew. Near the front door of the synagogue someone had painted a large *Fuck You*. There were recently scrubbed and white-washed patches all along the side of the building.

Music was coming out of the building, and I realized suddenly that it was Friday night. I felt a sudden urge to attend, to put myself into the company of living Jews. I pulled at the large doors, but they were locked. Forget it, I told myself: services had already started and besides, they obviously had security problems. I walked around the building in the darkness outside. Music, a faint chanting leaked into the night; I could see the silhouettes of hasids bobbing in prayer behind the windows, as if the place was filled with ghosts. The music stopped and I waited by the rear door of the attached Jewish Theatre building for the people to come out. When they did, I listened to their murmur of conversation until I heard people speaking English. I went over to the group and began talking to a couple, asking about the services, the synagogue, their trip. They were from Bethesda. They were seeing all the Jewish sites with a group, Auschwitz, Treblinka, the whole thing, they said. I began to tell them about my plans, about going to Kolno tomorrow. I went on. After a while I saw the husband glance uneasily at his wife and I realized that I was babbling out of a need not to be alone here. I shut up. An Israeli youth group—the kids all wearing light jackets with the word *Israel* embroidered on them—spilled out of the building, wisecracking, loud, cocky, arrogant: the kind of group I'd go out of my way to avoid in Israel. It was good to see them here.

When I got back to the hotel, I made arrangements to rent a car, and I bought a road map of Poland that was much more detailed than the one I'd brought with me. The map indicated regional tourist attractions with little colored icons of onion-domed churches, campers next to tents, fishermen, folk dancers in colorful ethnic costumes, horses-and-jockeys, hunters dressed like the gypsies in Dracula, wildlife: eagles, stags, boar, buffalo. There were no little pictures to indicate massacres, only a map symbol, a small black cross to mark what the legend called "martyrological sites." Kolno looked to be about 200 kilometers northeast of Warsaw: one took Highway 18, the Bialystok highway, to Ostrow Maz, a left turn north onto 63 to Lomza, and the possibility of two small, unnumbered side roads, one just north of Lomza going northwest, the other about twenty kilometers north at Stawiski, then a turn straight left, west to Kolno. The picture nearest Kolno was of a peasant couple, the woman in a full, wide embroidered dress and boots, the man dressed Cossack-style: fur hat, long flared out coat, boots. The couple was standing partially on an amoeba-shaped blob of green which indicated forest—the Piska—and partially on a field of small blue lines to indicate marsh or swamp.

RUMORS: ALTAR

The scream forms a silver knife in my grandfather's dream, cuts a cord in him, and he tumbles awake. As if his mind is still caught in the motion of his dream, he rolls out of bed and pulls on his clothing and his boots. Sitting on the edge of the bed, he is no longer sure if the scream was real. He thinks he should get up and check but is reluctant to face another crisis. If he goes back to sleep, perhaps it will dissolve. He rubs his face. His wife, my grandmother Sarah Gittel sleeps uneasily, muttering, her face, nested on the blood-stained feathers spilling from the ripped pillows, twisted into an expression of bitter triumph. Perhaps the noise was from a wild animal. Foxes and boars were coming out of the forest at night now, into the ruined streets of the town, sometimes even wolves, more of these now; they were developing a preference for human flesh. He has heard people have been attacked but doesn't believe it likely: the wolves could find enough fresh human carrion without having to endanger themselves. Watching the bloody feathers stirring under his wife's breath, he remembers the stories his father had told him when he was a child about Chmielnicki, the Cossack Hetman, and his massacre of the seven hundred Jewish communities. His father had spoken of these things with a kind of strange tenderness, a comforting tone, as if to reassure him that the days when men were beasts had safely passed into stories.

The scream pierces the air again. This time Sarah Gittel sits up, her cry echoing and trailing out the howl from downstairs.

Be calm—he's probably only having a bad dream, my grandfather says. He gets up and goes out through the salon, wincing at the bullet-torn, ax-splintered wreckage of their furniture: the samovar his grandfather had given him dented into junk, the upholstered sofa he'd transported from Danzig slashed, stuffing hanging out of its wounds, the Belgian carpet covered with mud and blood stains, the gutted clock. Wallpaper, damaged by the rain and snow coming in through the broken windows, hangs in soggy, fleshy strips from the walls. Sarah Gittel has not allowed him to clean any of this wreckage.

He walks into the children's room. My mother is standing over her brother's bed, patting his head with a damp cloth. He smiles to see her.

Ruhule, he says. Let me look.

He lights a candle next to the bed. Yitzhak moans as my grandfather picks up his hand, Pinhas noticing, not letting his daughter see him notice, the amount of blood that has dripped on the floor and bedding. When

Yitzhak was wounded last month, he had treated the injury himself, afraid to go to the Polish clinic The world is insane, the way we live in it, his other son Dov had said. That's neither here nor there, my grandfather said. *Nichstihier, nichstihein.* Now the wounded hand lies palm up on the sheet, gushing blood into a pattern, writing an accusation. He leans closer and sniffs. The blood smells bad. Get clean linen, more water, he says to my mother. Boil the water.

Papa, there's no wood.

Smash something. Use the clock. Do what you can, child.

His son must have torn out the stitching he'd done. The thumb is mashed and nearly off, not healing. The small torn tab of flesh tears at his heart: its vulnerability taking his mind to the quick dart of the mohel's knife at Yitzhak's circumcision, the answering tingle in his own flesh, a connection of his maleness to his son's, the wounds that bind them to a covenant of cuts and lost pieces. He thinks of his son Dov who had cut off two toes to escape from being pulled into the army. From which army was this boy escaping? My grandmother and my mother come into the room. Sarah Gittel draws in her breath sharply.

Murderer, she says.

For an instant he sees how he must look to her, tall and bearded in moon and candlelight, hovering over the broken form of his son.

Just help me. Later reproach me for my life.

She is holding the last of the Shabbat candles in one hand, linen samples he'd smuggled before the fighting in the other. My mother comes in with a bowl of water. He washes the wound again, Yitzhak moaning in fever and pain. Sarah Gittel picks up the hand and holds it while he rewraps it.

I must get him to a doctor. The blood may be poisoned.

I thought you were doctor enough, Sarah Gittel says. Doctor smuggler—you should have smuggled us away. What will you do now: make a doctor out of a column of snow, breathe life into its nostrils?

Hoffman's on the other side of the border.

On the other side of the moon.

He finishes wrapping the bandage. For a few seconds, the thumb is hidden by the white, pure linen. But, as he watches, a spreading spot of red brings out the pattern of the weave. He starts to unwrap the wound.

Get your needle and thread.

Cholera, my grandmother curses.

She leaves the room. In a few moments she comes back with the wooden box in which she keeps her sewing things. She holds up a needle to the candlelight and threads it, squinting, ties it off, then looks impatiently at her daughter.

What are you studying me to learn? Go to the kitchen and bring the bottle of vodka your father hides there. I've shown you where it is.

When she comes back, my grandfather uncorks the bottle and takes a drink in front of his wife's eyes, then pours the vodka over Yitzhak's hand. The boy screams. My grandfather sees a pure white spur of bone in the center of the wound, before the blood wells in again.

Pour, scoundrel, Sarah Gittel says. You'll get more.

He pours. Hold his wrist, he tells her. She holds it tightly, staring into his eyes. But when he brings the tip of the needle to his son's skin, his hand trembles. Without a word of reproach, Sarah Gittel takes the needle from his fingers. He pours, she sews. Her hand doesn't tremble. He feels a surge of love for her, then hate, each quickening his blood in the same way.

Strapped chest and shoulders to the sled, he pulls his son through the Piska forest. The runners break heavily through the crust and resist his pull; he's wrapped the boy with thick horse blankets over swaths of fine linen he smuggled from Danzig through this same forest. The wind twirls sparkling columns of snow up between the birch and pine trees; when he breathes deeply the icy air scratches his lungs. His breath, sparkling, dances like delirium in front of his eyes. Loud cracks boom from deep in the forest, trees exploding in the cold. Smuggler's weather.

Five versts, he thinks. To go on the road is impossible in any case. Bands of deserters are murdering travelers for food, clothing, the brief frictive warmth of rape. He knows where to go: this is the white crack between countries in which he moves. The snow mist swirls and wraps around his legs and up his body, veils the trunks of the trees so they seem transparent, ghosts of trees. He the consciousness in that swirling mist, its brittling breath, *Ruah*. The cold edges into the warmth of his lungs, a nuzzle of death. When he looks back he can't see the sled, only the rope he is attached to disappearing into blinding white.

He pulls against the weight, fighting its soft sinking into the snow. Beads of sweat form on his face, freeze and fall tinkling. The burning coldness he gasps into his lungs moves to his stomach, his heart: he feels his bones growing thin and brittle. Bird bones. He bends forward and draws harder and he is light and hollow boned as a bird and he lets the lightness flow back and hollow the rope, pass into the sled and its burden and he rises with it now in the swirling white cloud, into the sky, up and up until he is above the mist and can see it below, the black spear tops of the firs sticking out of its milky thickness and now the whole forest stretching below him, the church spire of the town, the market square teeming with men and women and animals embracing and bowing and jumping up and down in a strange dance, a pattern which only could be seen from above. He soars, carried up in a draft that pushes his chest and stomach like someone pressing a pillow up against him and at the top of his gyre he can see everything, the Prussian border to the north and west, the Russian border to the north and east, locked together like teeth; he flows in between, a human being smuggling his own human heart. He sees the cracks between nations swarming with dark bearded men, smugglers with glittering eyes, the gleaming, sea-salt crusted city of Danzig, the twisting streets and narrow alleys of Bialystok, the red domes of Moscow; if he soars higher he will see Jerusalem itself, a tawny city straddling mountains like a sleeping lion.

A tree, its black trunk glazed bright with ice, appears before him, spears him back to the earth. He pulls his frozen eyelids apart. In the slit he watches the tree bulge, the ice swelling in its veins. The tree splits with a loud crack as if sundered by an invisible ax; its insides show white as a bone in a wound. Who has ever seen such a sight? He kneels and picks up a heavy branch split from the exploded tree, to help him walk, to weigh him to earth. What a strange land I've been made a stranger in and must move in with this weight. Will You speak to me now with wonders and miracles from this tree that doesn't burn? What will You ask of me now for there's no mountain here and no altar and no ram to give in my son's place but You can't have him, this one, I'll walk on this earth with this one, You have enough of my children.

The whirling snow parts like a curtain and reveals a dim hulked shape fast against the base of a birch tree. Fear squeezes his heart but he moves closer. A tapered, gentle brown face forms, fur beaded with balls of ice, soft brown eyes open under cataracts of ice, spikes of ice hanging from the antlers, the stag leaning stiff against the tree, knees locked. *Tzaar baal hayim*, pity for living things. Nevertheless it is a miracle; he'd asked for a ram and had been given this, a life given instead of a life. He brings his face close, his breath stirring the fur, and stares into the animal's eyes. A flicker of warmth blinks into him, a hot corner of its soul.

Stop, a voice says.

He stares wildly at the deer, his heart beating.

Here, you bastard.

Here another miracle, a bear waiting against an oak next to the birch, its black matted brows and hairy face thick with ice, breath steaming from its red nostrils and lips. My grandfather comes closer, gripping the icy stick in his numb hand. The bear becomes a man, a deserter, or a wounded soldier left to freeze, sitting with one hand casually in his lap; the man growls at him. The man's right leg is outstretched in front of him at an odd angle from his body, the snow around it spotted red.

Come, brother, whoever you are, help me.

Sir, my son is hurt. I'm taking him to a doctor.

The man laughs, coughs like a bear. Where's his hospital—in a tree? Is he a bird? He peers brightly at my grandfather. *Zhid*, ain't it? What are you doing here, with your little *zhid* son? Is he on the sled? *Farshivy zhid*, he's dead by now, in this cold.

No.

The man laughs. He moves his hand, revealing a pistol in his other hand. Come closer, come on, bring the sled. Hurry up—no stalling. I'm starving and freezing, you son of a bitch.

The man has turned back into a bear. My grandfather, on the other hand, turns into a *farshivy zhid.* Fawning, craven. Harmless. The bear laughs with satisfaction. I asked for a ram, but a bear will do, my grandfather thinks as he swings the stick heavily against the matted jaw. The eyes widen and the mouth drops open in astonishment. He hits the head again and then again, the hardness of the skull giving and then softening. A cell of death moves up the icy stick and into his hand and arm.

He flips the body over, puts the gun in his coat pocket and strips off the fur coat and gloves. He brings them back to the sled and covers Yitzhak. Holding his breath, he uncovers Yitzhak's face. He puts his lips on his son's lips. Ice to ice. He stays, fastened, breathing into the boy until he feels a spot of warmth on his lips and closes his eyes and drinks his son's breath, its warmth moving through his body, flowing everywhere except into the arm and hand that had gripped the stick. They remain heavy as if full of ice. He takes off his other glove and grasps his skin there. It feels as if he's pinching the flesh of a stranger. He nods, understanding, a death instead of a death, another piece of himself clipped in exchange for a covenant. He begins moving again through the forest, earth bound, gripping the strap around his chest with his left hand, his right arm useless, dead as a frozen branch.

HIGHWAY 18

In the morning the car, a small red Renault, was delivered to the hotel. The Avis agent gave me directions to get out of Warsaw, and cautioned me to leave the car only in "guarded" parking lots at night: I'd have to pay for the protection, otherwise the car would be stolen or stripped. He asked me where I was going; when I told him he smiled at me. Polish roads, he said, were not like American roads, particularly out in the country. I didn't think they would be, I said. It should be an interesting trip, he said.

I managed to blunder my way out of Warsaw and onto the Bialystok road. Highway 18 consisted of a lane and a half on each side—what would be the shoulder on an American road was used as a traffic lane. The two directions were divided by a broken line: cars and trucks pulled into the oncoming lane frequently to pass, the etiquette seeming to be that if you were not the one passing but the one being rushed at head on, you got out of the way into the shoulder-lane on the right. It was a dance sometimes complicated by the custom Polish farmers had of letting their cows graze in the ditch next to the shoulder lane and the cows' custom of sometimes wandering out into the road, or by the peasants who would set up shop in that lane, calmly sitting and selling jars of mushrooms or other produce.

The countryside was in fact beautiful: golden stalks of wheat swaying in fields bordered by pine and birch forests, green meadows grazed by herds of cattle or sheep guarded by solitary storks, the road often shaded by tall, graceful cedar trees. As people do with scenery, I searched my mind for a comparison until finally it came to me: if you discounted the peasants driving ox carts and the storks, much of the countryside looked like Maryland, somewhat like the rural area where I live, but even more like western and northern Maryland: rolling hills and farms and forests. The farm houses and the older homes in the small towns were made of dark wooden planks, the newer homes of plaster and brick; there were thatch-roofed barns in the fields. There was beauty but no innocence. My first main reference point on the map in the journey northeast of Warsaw was Ostrow-Maz. Just south of it, an arrow pointing to a small road on the right, was a sign that said "Treblinka." Ostrow-Maz, the pivot on that road to the death camp, was a much smaller version of Warsaw, no large buildings, a suitably scaled-down massacre of local Jews—a few hundred people rounded up and machine gunned—that same mixture of a new commercial strip and drab post-war housing and a bright sprinkling of flower-decorated balconies and careful gardens and tile-roofed cafes, that same sense to me of physical normalcy as a mask, a body busily dancing on without its soul, a vacant grin on its face. The name of the town appeared on a sign next to the road, and the town attempted to present itself to me as simply a place behind that name, like the housing development laid on top of the Warsaw Ghetto, a place where people went about their existence.

And then I was tired of myself; I was driving through beautiful landscape in a new country and seemed determined to see only what was rotting under it, as if the road I was taking ran as a parallel dark dank tunnel under the earth. Yes, I told myself, and in Western Maryland there's Antietam and Sharpsburg, and in St. Mary's, where I live, archaeologists have found Piscataway Indian bones and artifacts going back thousands of years, and there are still slave quarters standing near my house, and the most beautiful beach and park in the area is built on top of a Federal POW camp where 3,000 Confederates died of disease, starvation and murder. Maybe if I were Indian or black or had an ancestor who'd died at Point Lookout I'd feel differently about St. Mary's. The past was buried everywhere like a murder victim, marked only for interested tourists under a black cross—when its bones came out of the earth they were quickly reburied or built upon or called something else, and I didn't have to always see them, write about them, sit on the porch with them in Boston, watch them squat grinning from the rafters. It was probably only a matter of travel anyway, that jar to the vision, that slight yank on the roots of perception that comes with changing places, with stepping out of the airplane and onto the tarmac, with watching the brass doors of the Holiday Inn elevator slide open and split my reflection just before I stepped through them, with walking up the street to the Ghetto, with driving into the Polish countryside.

The road passed out of the town and another sign appeared, the town's name again but now with a diagonal line slashed through it: ~~Ostrow Maz.~~

I turned onto a smaller road and followed it until I saw a fork and a sign for Lomza. I stopped the car and photographed that sign, as if it were evidence to prove a case.

KOLNO

On March 16, 1968 [Charlie Company] entered an undefended village on the coast of Central Vietnam and murdered around five hundred old men, women, and children in cold blood. The killings took place, part maniacally, part methodically, over a period of about four hours. They were accompanied by rape, sodomy, mutilations, and unimaginable random cruelties. "It was this Nazi kind of thing," we were told over and over by men who were there—an observation underscored by a single unassimilable thought: How could we have behaved like Nazis?
    —*Bilton and Sim:* Four Hours in My Lai

"If you licked my heart, it would poison you."

Rachel Alter-Borkowski, who grew up and had her family in Kolno, had gone back to search for surviving members of her family just after the war. "I made every effort to trace those nearest and dearest to me," she wrote. "Enveloped in a large shawl, I wandered about towns and cities...I did not reach Kolno that time. Gangs of bandits were roaming about...I was afraid to be recognized and killed." But just before she emigrated, she decided she had to go to Kolno "to visit my fore-fathers' graves for the last time." She writes of leaving Warsaw and reaching Lomza, where "all the houses in the old market square have been destroyed," the next day. When the Kolno bus arrives, she pushes on it. "A deep heavy pain is suffocating me. Everything seems unreal, Some mysterious life-power seems to be reviving in my heart the most secret memories. I cannot stop looking around, I imagine that soon I'll be seeing old Steinsapir or Brickman, the former bus owners..."

Lomza is a large town, obviously a regional center. The street I drove along was lined with dusty poplars and fronted with shops and restaurants and churches and drab brown apartment buildings with tiny, narrow balconies—nothing more really than fenced ledges. The physicality of the place, at least from the car, didn't evoke any of the history I was looking for. This town cropped up in family stories as the place people went to get away from Kolno's provincialism, and also as the town from which most of my Israeli relatives came. Lomza is mentioned a number of times in the Kolno Memorial book, though mostly in a peripheral way— asides in the survivors' accounts. Sosnow speaks of it as important to the trade in grain, cattle and horses because the nearest railroad station was there; there's also mention of a large yeshiva in Lomza. When Alter-Borkowsky wrote her description of returning to Kolno, she'd gotten the bus here.

I remembered Alter-Borkowsky's words as I drove by what seemed to be a main square, her mention of my maternal family surname, Brickman. A group of people, some holding plastic net bags and baskets filled with fruits and vegetables, were lined up at the bus stop: I saw a dusty sign for Kolno on the waiting shelter.

Dinah Koncepolsky-Chludniewitz, the Jewish woman who survived the massacre, also told of the end of the Jewish community in Lomza. She describes running away from Kolno "like a hunted beast" after the third German "action," in early August of 1941. "About fifty people [of 2,000] managed to escape," she writes, "but the majority were captured by farmers in the neighborhood who turned them over to the Germans." But she was given shelter by a friendly farmer, Michael Tcharnetski, a former customer of her father, who risked his life to hide her. Eventually, at her insistence, the good Tcharnetski took her to Lomza, where a ghetto had been set up by the Nazis. But having already lived through the stages of extermination in Kolno, she saw the signs in Lomza: "Decrees, murders of individuals, and mass actions indicated clearly that the end was near. The final extermination seemed a matter of days." In November of 1942 she ran away from the ghetto with ten other people who eventually joined another hundred Lomza Jews "who had escaped the night before the great slaughter."

It was afternoon and I didn't know how late I'd stay in Kolno, so I stopped and booked a hotel room near the square. Beyond the guarded parking lot of the hotel, the road went down a steep hill and over a river and I could see a postcard Eastern European vista: forests and villages and a lovely onion-domed church. I drove into it.

~~Lomza.~~

At Stawiski I saw the first road sign for Kolno. I photographed it, then turned left, west. The road became narrower, a small country road lined with cypress and pine trees, pastures dotted with cattle and sheep, and fields and forests stretching away from it. The only other vehicle I saw was a tractor that droned ahead of me for an instant before I passed it. I passed a number of hamlets, each too small to even be on the map: just a name on a sign, a cluster of ten or fifteen wooden, thatch-roofed houses like a picture book shtetl, the hamlet's name with a diagonal slash through it. This was the shortest leg of the journey, but time seemed to stretch until I imagined the road going on and on through this countryside, imagined driving for hours and days. My destination suddenly seemed impossible: how do you arrive at a story, a memory? I began to feel I was violating something in the fabric of time, and I understood, viscerally, why my cousins and my mother had refused to come back here. Let it lie.

Kolno.

And a sense of let-down after the sign, because the first building I saw was a small, balconied apartment building, Polish communist modern. Let down, but also relief that the town might be so changed as to be unrecognizable, just another Polish town.

The road went around a corner, up a hill and divided around a small tree-shaded park. The streets surrounding it were lined with shops and two story shingle- or tile-roofed brick buildings covered by yellow or mauve or brown or pale green plaster. There was a stone monument in the center of the park. The hand-drawn map from the Kolno book slid into place in my head. The market square.

I parked next to it, thinking: I'm parking next to the market square. I needed to keep putting what I was doing and where I was doing it into words in my mind or I would lose it into the stream of the everyday, where my mind was anxious to put it anyway. Looking down from the square to the south and to the west, I could see the forests and fields surrounding the village, like a physical anchoring to the past. The main street that bordered the western edge of the square continued on to the Lomza road, descending a hill past old brick and wooden buildings. A tractor drove by and there were a few people looking in the store windows: farm equipment, a beauty salon, a toy store, its cheap plastic figurines and cars and cap pistols covered with dust. Down another street I could see the high brown spire of a wooden church. I turned and walked into the small park. Old people sat quietly on the benches in the shade.

I walked to the monument in the center of the park, wondering if in fact what had happened here had been remembered and commemorated, if this had been where Lenin's statue was. The monument was a kind of obelisk; there was no mention of Jews on it, only a bas relief of an abstract, heroic soldier, the year 1945 engraved below him: a memorial apparently to the liberation by the Soviet army in 1945. And also to Ice-T whose name had been spray painted at the base of the monument.

"Why did the forest above them look so bright, the fresh blue sky appear so innocent?" Rachel Alter-Borkowski wrote. When she'd come back to the town and stood in this place I stood now, time had slipped in her mind:

I see them all, crowding together in the market square; I see their burning faces and their looks, frozen by fear.

I hear them being cursed, see them whipped and tortured.

I see the human animals around them, the hangmen's hard, indifferent faces, so degenerate and coarse that I turn away in disgust.

But all I saw now were the people sitting quietly on the benches, strolling in front of the shops around the square. It was a warm July day in Kolno and a breeze moved in the trees that had grown in the market square. The scene was too real for me; that is to say what was real in the scene could not be seen with the eye, could only be given life with the incantations of words stirred through memory and imagination, the stir of image and magic and time. Kolno lay in the sun, dead as a fact.

I walked out of the park and began taking photographs. People stopped to look at me. Three women sitting on a stoop stared and whispered. It was a small town, a farm town, and no tourists, no buses on the martyological route would come here: no black cross marked the spot on the map, only a happy peasant couple, their feet in a marsh. I began walking up and down the cobblestoned streets that sloped down from the market square. Many of the houses lining them could have in fact been here when my mother was a girl: houses of crumbling brick and yellow or lime green plaster, or crate-like houses of wood: the boards vertical in one, horizontal in another, painted blue or yellow or white or worn to blackened boards bowed with age and pressure, their window frames carved with designs. Some of the old wooden houses were small and cramped, their wood-shingled roofs buckling, but there were pleasant vegetable and sunflower gardens in back yards and everything was neat and clean. An old man swept the dirt in front of his house. A group of old men sat under the leafy shade of a trellis in front of a kiosk, playing cards and drinking. Everything seemed subdued and silent, but I had the feeling that a crowd of people was disappearing just as I came into sight. As I passed one yard, a German Shepherd leapt to the end of his chain, barking savagely, quivering and frantic with a need to get at me, my smell driving him into a tantrum of fury and fear. As if he knew who I was.

Avner Aliphaz went back in 1961 and wrote to a friend:

I went through the whole town...thinking of all the dear Jews who once lived here. The houses seemed to have bent down and blackened, as though mourning for their Jewish dwellers, who went away and never came back. I saw your house, too, in Lomzer Street...and the houses which belonged to the Bursteins, Rosenfelds, Lubels, Tsivyakovskis, Hurwitzes and Krelensteins. I saw them all. Christians were living in them...but never a Jewish face.

There were not even ruins now, nothing to tell me which of these houses might have belonged to the Rosenfelds and Lubels, whether the Brickmans had been nearby or where the Karlinskys lived.

I wandered. On the street that went to the Lomza road, I found an abandoned brick building that looked like an old railroad station: its windows were boarded shut. On my map it was in the place where the Yiddish theatre would have been. I took a photograph. People stared at me, but I didn't encourage them, only hid behind my camera. In Warsaw, I'd had the hotel desk clerk translate a list of questions for me: Were you here during the war? Where is the Jewish cemetery? The synagogue? Where were the Jews killed? Did you know the Brickman family? The Lubels, the Rosenfelds, the Karlinskys? But I hadn't been sure if I was going to try to speak to anyone and now I didn't want to. "How are you going to go about it?" Gloria Emerson, a writer who had done thousands of interviews asked me before I came. "Dear boy, don't be silly, you have to hire an interpreter. You need to talk to people. Otherwise what's the point?" But I didn't know what the point was, except to be here, and I wanted to be here alone. I wasn't here as journalist or writer or anything more than ghost now, a form that had driven the watch dog crazy, as if this was the formed point, the flesh and blood, finally come, of all the inchoate dread he'd always sensed in the humans of this town but had never seen or smelled or seen walking until now. On the Boston T my characters had come to life and intruded into mine; I felt I was the intruder now, as if I'd passed into the veil of stories. I didn't want to talk to anyone, not now; I didn't know what I would say or do.

I found the Catholic cemetery—Kolno's only cemetery now. It seemed to cover about five acres, fronted on one of the streets of the town. It was well and pleasantly shaded, the crowded graves marked with black or white crosses, some decorated with the iron spokes, like sun rays, I'd seen in other cemeteries I'd passed on the road. The Jewish cemetery, according to my map, should have been down the same street. One of my main goals was to find it; to find, if not my grandfather's headstone, at least some broken fragments that I could say kaddish over. In the photograph I have of his grave, one can make out two small stones placed on the base of the monument, following the Jewish custom of leaving stones on stones to commemorate a visit to the dead. And the cemetery was now more than simply the place where the bones of my ancestors were buried: the rubble of Lenin's statue would be there, the remains of the mock burial that had preceded the massacre of the community. The cemetery had gone in my mind from a symbol of continuity to a symbol of the restless murdered, a symbol of the uprooting of Kolno.

Rachel Alter-Borkowski hadn't gone there, but Avner Aliphaz had found the place in 1961 and said "a strange prayer, uttered by one who remained alive in honor of the souls of all our dear ones who have no one left to remember their name and light a candle to their memory." But the Jewish cemetery was gone, or I couldn't find it. As I walked down the street all I saw were more modern, concrete buildings: some sort of school, town offices, a discotheque. There was nothing to touch.

"Look," a Pole said to me—"here, in an open grave the Nazis killed Shepske the gravedigger...they forced him to dig his own grave and lay down in it. Then they shot him; the grave remained half-open...the gravedigger is no more; the book with the list of the Dead disappeared with him; how could you find anyone's grave?"

I walked back to the town center. If I wasn't going to speak to anyone now, I thought, there was nothing to do but go. The church, a lovely spired structure of dark brown wood, was just down from the square. In my mother's time it would have been an alien, menacing presence to the Jews, a constant reminder that majority or not they would always be uneasy, hated guests, a necessary evil, barely tolerated and sometimes not— Christ killers. But a priest might be more likely to be educated, to speak another language, to know something of the history of the town.

I entered the cool, vaulted building. It was empty and dark. I called out a hello, but no one answered.

Walking back to the market square, I saw an old lady, babushka around her head, sitting on the side of a grassy hillside with a child—probably her grandson. I smiled at her and she smiled back. O.K., I thought. She's old enough. Talk. I pointed to myself and forced a word out: "America." My lips felt wooden and numb and the word sounded strange; it was as if I were a monk breaking a vow of silence I'd kept for years. "Muter, vater—Kolno," I said. She looked surprised, but nodded encouragingly. "Zydowski," I said, Jewish, and peered into her eyes to see if there would be something, a flash of anger or horror that I could react to with my own anger or horror. But she just continued to smile and nod as if the word had become meaningless here. I knelt down next to her and took out my questions. I pointed at the one on the list that asked the location of the Jewish cemetery. Her finger moved along the line hesitatingly and her lips moved, forming the words—reading, I realized was difficult for her, if she read at all. I tried saying the words: she smiled and nodded.

I smiled and nodded back.

I got up and continued towards the market square. Three old men walked by me. On impulse, I caught up with them and started speaking, going through my mutter vater Kolno zydowski routine.

Two of the men looked away. The third stared at me. He pointed at me. "Kolno?" he said. "Familia?"

I gave him my mother's maiden name: "Brickman."

His eyebrows shot up. "Da, da," he said, and touched my face.

"Brickman, Brickman." He nodded. I felt light-headed. I wondered why he was using the Russian word for yes instead of the Polish. He waved around the square. "Famila Brickman," he said, nodding. He seemed excited. The other two men were still staring at me.

I pointed at a question on the list—where was the house?

He grimaced, shook his head.

Cementarz zydowski?

He made an erasing gesture. "Kaput," he said. Then he grinned at me and said: "Synagogue."

I stared at him. "Where?" I asked. He pointed away from the square, then tugged at my arm.

The four of us walked down a street from the square, around a corner, down another street. "Synagogue," the old man said. The Jews and all evidence of them were gone from the town, but this was a word he knew, that he still knew attached to the large three story building in front of us, its faded tan-pink plaster falling and peeling off in large jagged patches, so that the red brick underneath showed through like wounds. It took up about half a town block. Its doors were covered with iron grates and its windows blocked with either bars or rusting metal plates or boards—and several on the end bricked shut. Clearly the building was not used anymore. I wondered why. I hoped there were ghost stories, that the darkness inside was a well of unease for the town. I walked slowly around three sides of the building: the back was blocked by a fenced lot. On one side were sixteen square windows, seven on each of the first two stories and two on the top, under the peak of the roof. On the opposite side there were two large arched windows on the first story and two small rectangular windows under the peak. My cousin Bernie had told me that our family had sent money from America to donate a window to the synagogue when it was repaired in the thirties—one of the black and white photos I had showed that window. It was the shape of these arched windows; it could have been one of them.

I turned and saw the three old men staring at me. I nodded and thanked the man who had brought me. They left me alone.

I continued walking around the building, taking photographs. Next to it was some sort of Polish army motor pool: a soldier looked at me suspiciously.

I knelt at the base of the building. My hands worked at the plaster. It loosened and crumbled between my fingers and I drew away a lump of plaster and brick and a shard of brick and I put it into my pocket, thinking of the stones placed to commemorate a visit to my grandfather's destroyed grave. I'd leave nothing here—only carry away, as if in rescue.

Walking back towards the square, I noticed that there seemed to be more people in the streets now. I stared at them and they stared at me. I remembered seeing a film about a Palestinian woman, American educated, liberal, a believer in compromise with the Israelis, going back to Jerusalem and passing her old home, now occupied by a Jewish family. What she felt, she said, was pure hatred. I knew the analogy was inexact: the Jews here had been murdered, not driven out; this was never their country, and no Jew I knew had any desire to come back here. But the emotional analogy was true: at that moment I knew exactly what she had felt. The kind of numb disbelief and occasional horror I'd been feeling sharpened or focused into anger. That abandoned shell on a side street, unmarked as the market square, anonymous as the paved over cemetery—militantly forgotten. It was the anger one would have at seeing a murderer strutting free, wearing the clothes and jewelry of his victims. To forget was sometimes good, sometimes necessary. But this forgetting was obscene: what I'd come from had been erased, and even that erasure had been erased and denied.

When I got to the square it was calm and green, and a breeze still ruffled the leaves in the trees around the non-monument to the murders that had taken place here. My eyes suddenly blurred. I stood in the center and said a few words, all I could remember, of the mourners' kaddish, the prayer for the dead: "yitgadal, v'yitkadash, sh'ma rabah," those same four words, meaningless for me, but I said them over and over as if they were the only language for grief. I prayed that those who had died here and from here would be at peace and would know that I was here to remember them. I stared at the grass and trees and I made myself visualize how in this square babies had had their heads dashed against paving stones, how the mob of Poles and Germans had mocked and raped and beaten. How from here the soldiers had loaded Jews onto trucks and taken them to ditches and machine gunned them and I thought how the image that had come into my mind when I'd read that in the Kolno book, and that came into my mind as I stood here now, was a comparison that was painful to make but that I understood suddenly was the point from which my journey and my life as a writer had begun: the ditches at My Lai where people in my uniform and of my nationality and in my time and in my war had systematically and insanely raped and sodomized and mutilated and machine gunned into ditches five hundred old men and women and children in that village far from Kolno but forever connected to it, sharer of a history whose commonality was stronger and more terrible than the mere commonalities of geography and nationality.

...The Germans began to drag the Jews out of all the corners and hiding places, they shaved the old men's beards and beat everyone they could lay their hands on. I regret to say many Poles also took part in all this horror... Shimanski, nicknamed the "Beetle"...You probably remember the two Burak girls (Joelke's daughters). He killed them both in an attic and they were found with their throats cut....the Jews were ordered to undress and were machine-gunned...

....The training came to me and I just started killing. Old men, women, children, water buffalo, everything...They

was the enemy. Period. Kill...I cut their throats, cut off their hands, cut out their tongue, their hair, scalped them. I did it. A lot of people were doing it and I just followed...we almost wiped out the whole village, a whole community...do you realize what it's like killing five hundred people in a matter of four or five hours? It's just like the gas chambers—what Hitler did. You line up fifty people, women, old men, children, and just mow 'em down... said Vernado Simpson to Bilton and Sim, and that was the comparison that came into my head— because it had happened, because it had happened in my war, because everything in that war had led to it, because I was standing here now, compelled to make a journey as if I were a line completing a pattern written in my heart. I'd tried to sever myself from that comparison. Intellectually, just as with the analogy I'd made with the Palestinians, I understood the weakness in it. Logically, I could tell myself that at My Lai 500 had been killed in what was considered the worst American atrocity of the war; in Kolno over 2,000 had been killed in what was considered a small, almost casual "action," a tiny thread in the tapestry of murder. Logically, I understood that atrocities against civilians hadn't been limited to one side in Vietnam, and that while they were an inevitable result of the way we fought the war, they were at least officially decried and no part of a deliberate policy of extermination. I could tell myself that we went as Kennedy kids, as convinced as Isaac Babel and his Cossacks that we were doing good in the world. I could tell myself that I had never done what the American soldiers had done at My Lai; I'd walked through or flown over the war with a Jew's consciousness and there were many like me and there were many good commanders and good units, even in that bad war. I understood that the intellectual validity of the analogy was weak. But there it was.

And in Kolno that day, what I really wanted, deeply, more deeply than thought or words, wanted in the depths of my denying heart, was to be here in the market square holding the machine gun I'd once used— to be here then or maybe even to be here now, to feel that hard cold curve of trigger metal under my finger. What I wanted with all my heart was to be the gunner in Hugh Thompson's helicopter, Thompson, the good man of My Lai, who, seeing the massacre, related it in his mind to the images he'd seen of Nazis shooting people into ditches and landed between the soldiers and a group of villagers they were going to shoot and ordered his gunners to shoot the soldiers if they didn't back off and let him evacuate the Vietnamese. I came down in Hugh Thompson's helicopter, landed hard in the center of the market square before the rubble of Lenin's statue and I was between the Jews and the mocking, hate-filled faces in the market square and as my finger tightened on the trigger I could see that all of the soldiers among them were wearing my uniform and I knew I should have chopped the toes off my foot rather than go to that war.

"*I hear the children crying, the young women and girls groaning as they are raped and tortured; I hear the*

*old men praying, the screams of the degraded and
lashed...together with them I shout: Who will avenge our
blood?! I hope that you too, murderers, will know terror
and pain when you die! I hope that you never know love,
because you don't know what pity is!"* cried Rachel Alter-
Borkowski.

"*I won't forgive,*" said Truong Thi Le, a survivor of
My Lai. "*I hate them very much. I won't forgive them as
long as I live. Think of those children, that small...those
children still at their mother's breasts being killed...I hate
them very much...*"

How could a crime be forgiven if it is denied? I told
myself, and what came into my mind then was Le Minh
Khue's face and the vision I'd had of her filling bomb
craters with her bare hands, erasing the war and the
vision I'd had of her crouching under my machine gun
fire, and what I thought then was perhaps everything
was forgivable but only certain people had the right to
forgive. I'd traveled a great distance to get here and I'd
gone nowhere and I understood nothing more than how
it would go on and keep going on and never stop, that
for all the earth Le Minh Khue had pulled into the
ditches with her hands, the earth would still quiver with
the unquiet demanding dead.

One of the three old men I'd met was still in the
square: he'd been the silent one, the one whose face I'd
described as "stricken." Now, staring at me, his face
twitched with what? Horror? Hatred? Fear? Memory?
Had he been part of it, witnessed it, tried to stop it,
participated enthusiastically? What was I to him: a

ghost, a relative of the murdered come back to claim property, a sign the Jews would never forget, that they'd always send someone, generation after generation a day would come and a car would come and a silent man would get out and walk around and stand here and stare as I stared at him now? His face looked more stricken than ever, and the sickness deepened in it when I smiled at him and I thought: this is the reason I've come here, to see this face. I looked into his eyes and I smiled and walked away to the car and I got the hell out of there.

~~Kolno~~

LOMZA

"I felt the presence of those who used to live here. The whole square is swarming with human figures...I am with them, but somehow outside them."
—Rachel Alter-Borkowski

I spent the night in Lomza. After I got settled in the hotel, I wandered the streets for a time. As in Warsaw, the modern stores and restaurants and apartment buildings along the main street were a facade. Coming off it were streets lined with old buildings and churches: I passed narrow alleys that opened to courtyards squeezed between crumbling, stained walls. Dilapidated balconies hung over bumpy cobblestone pavement strewn with garbage and pooled with black, noxious looking puddles: the air inside dank with stale time. The description isn't fair: some of the old buildings lining the streets were lovely. But the courtyards stuck in my mind—they could have been Isaac Bashevis Singer's 10 Krochmalna Street in Warsaw (the real Krochmalna now built up with the same block-style apartment developments that covered the Warsaw Ghetto area.)

There was no trace of the Jewish community, though I didn't look very hard. I didn't want to look any more. I simply wandered, letting myself see and hear without thought. Crossing the street in the square in front of the hotel, I tried to see the small park there as merely a small park, nothing under its soil but stone. Two prostitutes in tight miniskirts joked loudly to each other while an old woman in a babushka looked down as she passed them. I went into a restaurant. It was decorated in red velvet and black naugahyde like a Fellini bordello without the satiric element: an exaggerated, hopeful decadence. I walked down the street, looking for a kiosk or grocery. But they were all closed. I went back to the hotel. In the restaurant there the menu listed my mother's dishes: borscht, cabbage soup, herring, *riba zydowski*—"Jewish fish," meaning carp, meaning gefilte fish. I ordered all of it. It wasn't even close, or rather was only close in the way a memory compares to the real thing.

In my room, narrow as a cell, I opened the window on the square and let the sounds and air come inside, then took a shower. In the bathroom mirror, my face had narrowed as if the flesh had caved in: my cheekbones and nose seemed higher, more prominent. Dark circles shadowed and sank my eyes. I saw the face of an old, hunted Jew.

RUMORS: HORSES

He dreams of horses. Wild and snorting, flanks quivering, breath spuming, they run through his nights as he runs through his days so he wakes feeling more tired than when he put his head down. Twice, before the war, he had accompanied shipments of Polish horses sent by the horse dealer Supchik to buyers in Germany and Russia; jobs reserved for only the best riders among the Kolno Jewish youth. The horses, nervous and skittish at the train journey, would calm when he spoke soothingly to them, clucked at them, touched their twitching flanks. Together they'd look at the alien country flickering through the opening in the planks. He slept in the box car with them, curled on straw and pressed by horse flesh; the steam from their sweat, their breath warming him.

Now he is often feverish or light-headed from hunger, and when the darkness comes in a strange city he feels himself losing the edges of his form as if he is dispersing into breath. In his dreams, he gallops across plains bright with blue flowers. On the trains, just before arriving at his destinations, he'd curry the horses' flanks as if scraping away their old lives. Now he's torn himself free from the inevitability of his life and is neither here nor there, *nichstihein, nichstihier*. The words echo in his head, sometimes a soft canter of hooves, sometimes harder, the clatter of wheels against rails. *Nichstihein, nichstihier*. The classic choice, the family anthem. But he feels cut loose from all the commitments of his life: family, politics, religion, even the need to make choices: should he go to America, Palestine, stay in the struggle here? He's died and been reborn. He drifts.

Not long after he'd left Kolno, an old woman in a small hamlet had spat at his feet and crossed herself when he'd come to her door asking for bread, a little water, and he'd been hit from behind and woken up bound and on his back near the village well. The blow had been so hard he'd been shifted into detachment. He watched a flock of geese flying, the black V rippling through the white sky so that at first the black line of horses seemed to separate and emerge from sky, the horses growing larger and into their shapes and his heart swelled for here were all the horses of Kolno he'd fed and tended and whispered to coming for him in a luminous cloud to sweep him away from here and into the sky and he didn't move and now they were close enough he could see the streaming manes and long black and brown faces, flaring nostrils, specks of spittle flying, hooves flurrying the white dazzle of snow into a webbing mist so the horses were concealed and broke

through the white membrane again and now he could
see the long lean faces of riders, their white breath
spuming into the mist. Rifle shots cracked in the air.
Screams came from the village. Tongues of flame licked
at the sky. The village crackled. A bald, stooped Cossack
in rimless spectacles was holding a skinny pig up by its
snout, fingers in each nostril, the pink body stretching
towards the weight in its hips, the feet kicking. The
Cossack carefully slit its throat. The old woman who
had spat at him was lying in the mud with her throat
cut, another pig working at her frantically with its
snout, grunting and slurping at her neck and he looked
away, not disgusted but because he didn't believe in the
balance of perfect justice. A thin Cossack reared up next
to him and dismounted from the back of a roan stallion
as if he were unsheathing himself. He drew a saber and
cut the bonds, but kept the point pressed.

Why were you trussed? The thin Cossack asked in
Russian. Are you a gift?

I came looking for food. They might have thought
I was a spy. They knew I was a Jew.

Are you a spy for us?

I don't know who you are. I think you're a dream.

On the contrary, we're the Ninth Cossack regiment.

He laughed. The idea that these apparitions,
instrumentalities of his tilted mind, were numbered
struck him as hilarious. The flames eating the village
leapt around him like madness, crackling with his
laughter. The horses whinnied.

Of what army? he asked. The army of dreams?

Exactly. We're red cavalry.

The roan lowered his head and looked at him with its wise liquid eyes. It nudged him gently and whinnied softly. He kissed the horse's warm forehead.

The thin Cossack smacked his lips as if something tasted good.

That saves you, he said.

TREBLINKA

I drove south from Lomza and south of Ostrow Maz I
turned off the highway and followed the signs to
Treblinka. The villages I passed through were again
pristine and there was even more forest in this region
than around Kolno: the pines and oaks and birches
seemed taller and thicker, the forest darker: a good
hiding place. After the revolt at Treblinka, after the
prisoners had killed guards and blown up the gas
chambers and crematoria, some 200 of them had
escaped to the forest: of those only 40 survived the war.
To the left of the road, paralleling it, I saw a line of
railroad tracks and again realized that anywhere else
that thought would simply end. Not here. I was driving
alongside railroad tracks, the road following the tracks
to the town and the death camp of Treblinka. I drove
along through meadows dotted with goldenrod and lush
with clover: patches of undulating yellow waving on the
green. In the fields, the scarecrows had black hoods
placed over their heads.

There were only a few other cars on the narrow two lane road. At Malkinia a sign stated "Treblinka—7 kilometers." "Certain numbers," Hemingway wrote "...and certain dates and these with the names of the places were all you could say and have them mean anything."

And suddenly I am on the narrow bridge crossing the river Bug and the track suddenly becomes the road: I am on the railroad tracks going to Treblinka. I feel their cross ties bump under my tires and see the two lines of their rails meet at a perspective point in front of my windshield, a point of arrival on the horizon. Past the bridge, I see a line of old abandoned boxcars parked along the tracks. Skeletal: boards ripped, holes in their sides; they're rusting in the sun. There is no sign of a memorial: the cars are simply here. The obvious question comes into my mind. I stop and pull off the road and get out. There is no one here, only a buzzing silence in the air: it's a hot summer day on the tracks just outside Treblinka. The rotting blackened wood on the outside of the cars feels warm: the insides are dank and cool. I look for—what? Signs of clawing, carved initials? I look for signs. There is only the line of boxcars on the track in the sun. A photographer I knew had asked me to bring him a stone from Poland: he collected stones from different places: he said he felt a type of power in these objects. Or something. I take two stones from the railroad bed and put them in my pocket. I wonder what he will feel.

There were two camps at Treblinka. The first was a punitive labor camp that held both Jews and Poles who worked at the local gravel mine and at loading and unloading boxcars at the Malkinia station. Punitive labor meant that the camp's sole purpose wasn't extermination: there were no gas chambers. Of the 20,000 slave laborers at Treblinka I, about half died—of torture, beatings, shooting or starvation.

Treblinka II was built in the spring of 1942 solely as a death camp: its only reason to exist in the world was to exterminate Jews.

The camp covered some fifteen hectares and only Jews were allowed to build its interior: they of course would be killed anyway. There is intrinsic in this fact the implication that the Nazis—working in a partnership they didn't even know, but must have hoped would exist with modern Holocaust deniers—were immediately attempting to revise history: no one who worked on the camp was expected to survive it. In fact, after the camp was completely enclosed by a three meter high barbed wire fence, the Jews were made to entwine a screen of pine branches in the wire so that what was happening in the camp couldn't be witnessed from outside.

As soon as Treblinka was ready in July of 1942, a year after the Jewish community in Kolno had been massacred, transports of Jews began to arrive both from the Warsaw Ghetto and from all over Europe. They were met by the sight of a make-believe railroad station inside the camp, complete with signs for fake waiting rooms and other destinations.

After arrival, men and women were separated, made to undress and told by loudspeakers that they would be going to the showers and would receive new documents and clothing afterwards. Men, women and children were then herded naked to the gas chamber—they were packed inside, their arms lifted to squeeze in as many as possible:

Children were thrown in on top of that human mass. The gassings with exhaust fumes took about fifteen minutes. The bodies of the gassed victims were then transported by a working squad of Jewish inmates to a place where special grates were prepared. The bodies were interspersed with wood and incinerated after being doused with an inflammable liquid.

It was the Jewish workers, the *sonderkommandos*, who carried out the uprising. On August 2, 1943, two years after the Kolno massacre—and after 800,000 people had been gassed at Treblinka—the sonderkommandos broke into the armory, grabbed rifles, pistols and grenades, and began shooting German and Ukrainian guards. They managed to burn down most of the camp and to kill some 85 guards. The survivors of the revolt fled into the forest. Afterwards, the Germans started to abandon the camp—by November of 1943 they had destroyed the remaining "evidence" and planted trees over the gas chambers and crematoria.

The parking lot in front of the visitors' center—a long concrete building with its front wall covered by blow ups of photographs and documents—was empty. A young woman was reading a book in the information booth. She handed it to me and then gestured at a narrow road made of irregular stones that led behind the building, to the site of the camp.

I was absolutely alone.

I walked along the narrow road, the worn, round tops of the stones embedded in the earth pressing into my shoes, my feet caught and tugged as they slipped into the spaces between. It branched to the left and I followed it past the tall pines planted by the Nazis over the ruins of the camp. Long concrete blocks, placed parallel to each other like railway ties, bordered the path. The symbolism seemed unnecessary. The journey, my hunger and thirst and solitude in this place, were all working on me. I felt a stir in the base of my skull, a clamor of voices buzzing inside my ears. A large clearing opened to the left.

The memorial the Poles have erected here is more effective and moving than the heroic statuary at the Warsaw ghetto site; it stirs a sense of loss in the spirit the way the suggestive abstraction of the Vietnam Memorial does, a grief you don't feel staring at statues of idealized warriors in dramatic poses. In the center of the meadow where the camp had been was a Stonehenge-ish monolith with a menorah in bas relief on its side. Surrounding it, in a bordered circle and in scattered groupings all over the huge field were stones, hundreds of thousands of silent standing stones: a symbolic cemetery, the stones upright but uncarved, each with its own height and shape: jagged, angular, rounded, small, large, as if the erased cemetery at Kolno and all the other erased cemeteries had pushed back out of the earth.

Near the center monolith was a monument over one of the crematoria: a mound of black stones, its top a melted, agonized moonscape: the suggestions of hands, fingers, faces with their mouths open in silent frozen screams emerging from between the stones at its base.

I walked back, still alone, to the entrance, but instead of going out I doubled back along the right branch of the embedded stone road, It was the "black road," constructed by the prisoners from Treblinka II to the slave labor camp. I walked on the stones. I was sure there was a statistic somewhere, how many lives per mile, per yard, per foot it had cost to place these stones here. It was hot, the sun beating down and my throat was parched, but suddenly it became a point to not turn back, to walk to the end: what a self-indulgent, infinitesimal drop of discomfort to give, to flick into the pools of agony here—another symbolic fucking gesture. But I couldn't stop walking. Or I only stopped when I went to the side and squatted and let my fingers sink into the soft earth in which the stones were embedded. I sifted it through my fingers: ash; these stones were socketed into the ashes of the dead. I pulled a small red stone out from the gentle counter-pull of the ground: its bottom half was black with ash.

I walked, my eyes down on the stones. In many places they were fitted haphazardly together, as if in haste, under blows, yet in other places there were attempts at symmetry, at real workmanship, as if some Bridge on the River Kwai craftsman's pride had seized a single slave or a work gang and they had decided to leave their mark.

About a kilometer down the road, I saw Hebrew letters engraved on a number of broken stones mixed in with the others: gravestones uprooted from somewhere and used to pave the road: this was the place where the cemeteries and their gravestones and the stones left by the dead on the gravestones had gone; this was the place of stones.

"The aim of the (Treblinka) revolt," DePres wrote, "was to ensure the memory of that place, and we know the story of Treblinka because 40 survived...like any witness, the survivor gives testimony in situations where moral judgment depends on knowledge of what took place."

At the end of the road I knelt down and took two loose stones and put them in my pocket, next to the shards of brick I'd taken from Kolno.

RUMORS: STRENGTH

It is sometimes for my mother as if she's become a small girl again, lying at her father's side and twining the wiry curls of his beard while he caresses her hair, and sometimes it is as if her father has become her child, lying helpless, his eyes wide and amazed, his other arm stiff at his side. The house is so cold their breaths are visible, twisting in the air. Above their heads are the potatoes, the only charity Sarah Gittel allows the family to take. My mother tries to imagine she and her father are under the earth, the roots of plants growing over and around them, closing them in a living center of warmth, or that they are still hiding underground holding each other as they had when gentile armies clashed in the streets of the village and Polish neighbors came looking for Jews.

Hunger pinches her insides and throat. After her father's stroke, a small delegation of women from the Jewish Women's Aid Society had come to the house. Sarah Gittel opened the door and stood on top of the concrete stoop, cold and thin-faced in her black silk dress. She'd stared, her mouth a tight closed line, as they'd talked softly to her until my mother, watching from a window, could see her silence spread over them, one after another. Finally, they looked at each other, turned and walked away. Sarah Gittel closed the door without a word. The next morning, a basket of potatoes had been left anonymously on the stoop. Another had appeared each Shabbat. Who knows where potatoes come from, Sarah Gittel said, taking them inside.

Eating potatoes, selling them in the market square are all that keeps them alive. Her brother, Yitzhak, is feverish, his wound refusing to heal; her father's right arm is frozen at his side, his voice frozen in his throat. He grunts and emits desperate trapped sounds that break her heart and make her mother turn away with a kind of satisfied disgust.

In the center of the market square in front of the house, a new Polish flag flaps in the wind, replacing the German flag that had replaced the Russian flag, who needs to travel? Every morning, my mother piles the sled with charity potatoes and sells or trades what she can, standing amid the burned and smashed stalls.

But who can buy anything? In the afternoon, Wanda, the daughter of the wet nurse Yasha who had suckled mother the first five years of her life, comes to look at the potatoes. She picks one up, then another, weighing each in the palm of her hand, examining each closely.

They're potatoes, Wanda, my mother says.

You'd better be careful, Wanda says. Dogs bark. Who are jealous. Who growl about a house full of treasure that they somehow missed during the pogrom. Whisper about a dead man in the forest, on the smugglers' route, hidden gold.

My mother points to the blackened potatoes.

Here's our gold, Wanda, all we have.

Peasants grow potatoes, Jews grow money, Wanda shrugs.

My mother thinks of the money her brothers Herman and Max had sent from America, growing under the floorboards, and flushes.

Your mother, for example, Wanda says, a woman who could pay someone else to be her breasts.

It made me your sister.

A sister who took milk from my mouth.

My mother stares at her. Wanda stares back, tossing her blond braids defiantly. Another changeling of this winter, a new flag.

When she tells of her conversation with Wanda, Sarah Gittel stares at her with burning eyes, a mocking expression of amazement on her face, as if to say: and this surprises you?

Why did you give me to Wanda's mother?

So you wouldn't suck me dry.

Mama, we have money.

American money. Dream money.

We can spend it.

Only for what its intended. She pats the handkerchief she keeps always pinned inside her blouse. In it are the two toes her son Dov had chopped off his own foot. Sarah Gittel is going to bring them with her if they go to America.

We can't eat what's left of Dov.

Sarah Gittel brings her face close. Her breath stinks coldly of potatoes.

Then be a stone. Stones don't need to eat.

She gestures upstairs, at her husband's room.

We have enough to leave. But can we put that weight on a sled and drag it after us?

Be quiet. He may hear. He protected you like a queen all your life.

Queens don't sit in the dark, eating rotten potatoes. Are you his wife now, to protect him?

That night when my mother lies in her bed, next to her groaning brother, she yearns to assume the delirium of Yitzhak's fever. It is a way to fly. Fly to America, a place where all shapes are possible. Dov is on his way, perhaps he is there already. He had put his bare foot on the stump outside and chopped off two of his toes to avoid being taken by the Czar's army; when they were going to arrest him anyway he'd flown, light and unanchored. She understands his need to escape, the swift chop of the ax, the quick, necessary severance from the trap. Yet her father had been felled by a stroke, as if struck by the arc of the same ax. As if it were swinging back and forth, swiping away the men in her family: Yitzhak injuring his hand and his flesh starting to rot, festering from the dirt and damp of the earthen cellar in which they'd hid during the pogrom. Her father had dragged him in the sled to a doctor, pulling him mid-winter and mid-war through thick crusts of snow in a forest of black frozen branches, full of wolves, bandits and deserters. He'd brought Yitzhak back with his son's hand cleaned and stitched, saved, but with his own coat stiff with blood and his own right arm frozen and dead, as if given in trade. My mother thinks for the first time in years of her sister Bechele, carried away by the flu. She had been struck first, before Bechele, burning with the fever that had taken away half the children of Kolno. She'd felt her soul already slipping out, light as a silken thread, unraveling her into mist. But her sister had come to her in that mist and smiled and touched her forehead, and she felt the thick hot worm of the sickness loosen from her heart. That night Bechele had taken to her bed and never rose. The smile was still on her face, left behind, better than toes, a clipped wing.

Papa, what should I do, where should I go?

You're not a stone. Fly.

I'm not a bird either.

You're my daughter, a smuggler's daughter. There are secret paths through the forest, I'll tell you about them. May He who blessed Sarah, Rebbekah, Leah and Rachel, Miriam the prophetess and Esther the Queen, Master of the World, may he bless you. Hazak v'et hazak. *Strength and more strength.*

The voice is so strong in her head she has to go to her father's room. He lies staring at his dead arm as if it were alien flesh grafted to his shoulder. He turns his stare to her. *Papa, where should I go?* His pale face glows in a patch of moonlight, eyes dark holes above a dark beard. The lips freeze into a rictus smile. The arm, twitching like a wing, begins to rise. Higher and then higher. My mother watches as he gathers himself and pulls his arm out of the sleeve of death. The moonlight bathes it. The fingers curl into a claw, slowly straighten. Point out of the window, to the moon.

CONNECTIONS

That day in My Lai, I was personally responsible for killing about 25 people. Personally. Men, women. From shooting them, to cutting their throats, scalping them, to...cutting off their hands and cutting out their tongue. I did it...It just came. I didn't know I had it in me...after I killed the child, my whole mind just went...And once you start it's easy to keep on. Once you start...I just killed. It can happen to anyone. Because, see, I wasn't the only one who did it. Hung 'em, you know—all type of ways. Any type of way you could kill someone, that's what they did. And it can happen.—*Vernado Simpson*

The [German] woman, put down her fork and interrupted me aggressively. "What is the point of all these trials they're having now? What could they do about it, our poor soldiers, if they gave them those orders? When my husband came on furlough from Poland, he told me: 'Almost all we did was shoot Jews, shoot Jews all the time. My arm hurt from so much shooting...'"—*Primo Levi*

I returned to Warsaw from Treblinka. In the Nozyk Synagogue I met a young Dutch woman who was showing the building to a couple who worked at the embassy: she spoke Polish and English. We spoke to the curator, a tall, thin proud-looking man who would not say much about how he survived the war but who told us that the synagogue had come through because the Nazis had used it as a stable—it was restored in 1983. He talked of massacres and desecrations and statistics: 3,000,000 Polish Jews killed, only a few thousand left, mostly old, mostly living now in Warsaw—a terrible spiel made more horrible because it had so obviously worn smooth in his mouth: the synagogue existed on donations. I could see the Dutch struggling to keep fixed to the idea that the statistics were real, to ignore the feeling that this was a hustle. I asked him about the graffiti and the spiel stopped and his face grew angry. They did it every night, he said, the Skins; he would wash the marks away and the next day they would be back, like something appearing out of the stone...the rabbi had been beaten up by Skins the year before, his beard shaven; he himself had been beaten. They waited outside, he said, and asked if he was Zydowski—when he said yes, they beat him. He made a fist, his knuckles big and jagged, and pressed it against his forehead to show us.

I left Poland the next day. By late afternoon, I was back at Heathrow. I went through customs and rushed to catch the Picadilly Line. I'd take it to Hammersmith, get out and cross the street, then catch the Hammersmith and City line to Royal Oak. My brother and sister-in law's apartment, where my wife and son were staying, was only a few blocks walk from there. I'd simply reverse

the routes I'd taken to leave for Poland. There was
something comforting in running through the pattern
in my mind, naming points and connections, as if it
were necessary to complete the journey. A magic
formula. I found a seat and rested my forehead for a
moment against the sticky vibrating window glass. The
darkness of the airport access tunnel flowed by; then we
were out of it. When I was a boy I'd enjoyed science-
fiction stories built around the time paradox: the
spacefarer who travels at the speed of light and returns
after a few years of his time to find hundreds of years
have passed on earth. It felt the opposite of that now, as
if I'd aged years in the short time I'd been gone. The trip
had had the temporality of a book, read in hours,
encompassing years. The country outside the window
looked leached. Scenes drifted over it: the apartment
buildings pressed over the bones of the Ghetto, the lush
camouflage of grass and trees growing over the market
square in Kolno; the black, spray painted word *Slayer!*
appearing on the wall of the building across from it like
a scream from the past oozing through the plaster.
Oroborous memories looping back endlessly into
themselves, sights and sounds and faces stirring into
stories I'd heard or that I knew I would create, into other
faces, memories, into my imagination, my attempt to
nudge the world into a pattern of points and
connections that I only saw was there after I'd created it.
In a word, into fiction. And I wondered again if in my
attempt to save lives, I wasn't simply killing them all
over, murdering their memory. Murder memory. The

noise and motion of the train made it into a chant. I looked out of the train window at the neat English houses passing by, small villages, stations. Connections.

"The station is Shepherd's Bush," the p.a. on the train announced. "Mind the gap."

Six months later I walk through the Holocaust Museum. Its macabre facts pile up, one after another, moments of terror preserved: the Nazi charts of racial types, a tilted clandestine shot of naked women about to be herded into a gas chamber, a shivering Jew being slapped by a soldier, filmed scenes from ghetto streets, scenes filmed by the Allied troops who liberated the camps, the scale model of gas chambers and crematoria and plaster Dantesque crowds of naked, writhing, agonized figures—perverse Disney, a grotesque small world after all. Facts made visual and all as horrible and finally as numbing as the litany recited by the curator of the Warsaw synagogue: they pound me into blankness, leave me only with an abstract admiration for the logistics and architecture of the place, the art of it, arranged and representational. Perhaps in its attempt I see the suggestion of my own defeat.

"It's too big, too American," my wife says—what moves her finally is the room full of nothing but piles of victims' shoes, layers and layers of them lying heaped on each other, tongues flapped out, the old skin of their leather cracked and mummified, their laces entwining with each other, but something in me steps back again and sees the pile as real but roped off and placed and selected: the facts of the shoes mixed with the perception of the creator of the exhibit. A group of teenagers is giggling and flirting in front of a wall-sized photograph of naked corpses packed into and spilling out of boxcars, and instead of being angry at them I find myself simply relieved to see them going about the business of life. They understand that they are in a museum. It needs to be bigger, not smaller. The laces need to grow out like vines, break through the roped-off area, extend and entangle.

But there is one exhibit that pulls me into itself, almost literally: a high-ceilinged room hung on all its walls with photographs from the daily life of a Jewish community, just like Kolno. We walk into this exhibit, you and I, as we walk into Kolno, into a book about Kolno, school trips, weddings, family gatherings, grinning students, woodcutters, flirtations, picnics. Individual faces and scenes surround us as if they are our own memories, in the way stories become memories. The utter normality of the poses and activities haunt us because we know the future these people in the photographs don't know, the final black ditches that will suddenly be drawn across the continuity of their lives and that will spread like shatterline cracks through distance and time and across the lives of millions of others. The photographs resonate with what we're not shown but that we know will happen, in the same way we read a story, let's say, about a pogrom in Kolno and people hiding in a black hole and we think about what they don't know: how that pogrom and the hate that engenders it are only the seeds that will bloom terribly in July of 1941, and perhaps we even think about a man, a descendent of those people who will walk years later on the same ground and think of them and of the massacres of newer wars. The murdered of Kolno lace with the murdered of My Lai, the faces spawn other names: Treblinka and Sand Creek, Deir Yassin and Ma'alot, My Lai and Cambodia, Bosnia and Rwanda, a world cracked with black ditches: the museum needed to be bigger; there needed to be signs to more corridors, signs to tell us where to go from here and where not to go, and without that the faces are lost, and we will have nothing left but the numbing hugeness of the crime, the categorization of facts,or worse: simply the license of example. We look, let's say at a photograph, let's say the photograph of three people and a grave we looked at when we started this journey, and through our imagining we remember those lives, our memory edged by the future that we know waits like a wolf; our joining memory gives us the word we can cry out in warning, tells us where the paths through the forest lead and which ones we need not take anymore. The journey, like all journeys, like all stories, was a tangle of connections and extensions and junctions, of seeing the image, the scene, the person, the ground, of seeing what radiated from the image, where it had come from, where it might go.

Once I'd sat on a porch in Dorchester with a small group of Americans and Vietnamese who had years before tried to kill each other and who now huddled together, laughing with the miracle and the hope of us sitting together, drunk with each other's presence as if we needed some proof of our own past; all of us as afraid of forgetting what we needed to remember as we were of remembering what we needed to forget. All of us willing to call it what it was and drink it anyway and write endless books and poems that try to break the droning spiel the past is being smoothed into and form it into a jagged fist that we can feel pressed against our own foreheads, that we can press against your forehead until a light bursts behind your eyes.

EPILOGUE

DECEMBER, 1994

A year later, hung-over and lazy and easy, I float with Le Minh Khue and another group of Vietnamese writers, veterans of our war, in a dragon-prowed boat along emerald paths of water threading through the maze of three thousand islands that stretch for 1,500 miles across Ha Long Bay. The day is misty and the great unearthly carboniferous chalk islands, pointed and worn as mossy teeth, loom darkly out of the water, dwarfing the boat. Their sides are vertical cliffs, carved with caves and grottoes: jade and ivory sculptures.

The day brightens. I fight the temptation to idealize or romanticize, to turn into metaphor. Fat chance. The islands float on perfect reflections of themselves in the water, *nichstihein, nichstihier,* sampans gliding between them like dreams. There is no line between illusion and reality. The emerald tendrils lead us between towering cliffs to places of unutterable loveliness and stillness or twist to dead ends or to the dangers of sharp rocks. You could drift into this place, lured by its beauty and driven to define it, control its mystery; you could get lost in its caverns and watery mazes; you could fall into the illusion that simply by wanting the ache of its beauty so much, it will be whatever you want it to be; you could still be drawn deeply, inextricably into it, as into love. It is a place my grandfather might have dreamt, a smuggler's dream.

And Hanoi moves out of the war and into a dusty, luminous morning of tree-shaded streets and rusting iron balustrades and people hunched on their low stools and benches outside the sidewalk food stalls where *pho*, the everything soup, thick with noodles and chunks of yellow chicken or pork or blanched beef, is bubbling in black pots on the charcoal stoves that sit next to golden masses of noodles and piles of bean sprouts and green scallions and skewers of pork frying on braziers. And I sit and watch clouds of blue charcoal smoke veiling and then revealing the old ochre colored walls streaked with soot and age, and my companion takes my chopsticks and wipes them carefully and thoroughly before handing them to me, a gesture that stirs me unexpectedly close to tears of gratitude or grief, that suddenly seems part of a ceremony performed to bring something to its close.